THE
AVENGERS
A CELEBRATION

THE AVENGERS

A CELEBRATION

50 Years of a Television Classic

Marcus Hearn

TITAN BOOKS

For Amanda, who always had M appeal

ISBN 9781848566729

Published by
Titan Books
A division of
Titan Publishing Group Ltd
144 Southwark St
London
SE1 0UP

First edition October 2010
10 9 8 7 6 5 4 3

Designed by Peri Godbold. Jacket designed by Martin Stiff.

Visit our website: **www.titanbooks.com**

Did you enjoy this book? We love to hear from our readers.
Please e-mail us at: **readerfeedback@titanemail.com** or write
to Reader Feedback at the above address.

A CIP catalogue record for this title is available from the
British Library.

Printed and bound in China by C&C Offset Printing Co., Ltd.

Acknowledgements

Thanks to Roy Ward Baker, Honor Blackman, Brian Clemens, John
Hough, Patrick Macnee, Julie Stevens, Linda Thorson and Leonard
White, who shared their memories of *The Avengers* with me.

The majority of the images in this book were scanned by Sharon
Ankin, and all were restored by Peri Godbold, Paul Taylor and myself.

Special thanks to Jaz Wiseman, who generously filled the spaces in
the picture archive and the gaps in my knowledge. Thanks also to Phil
Belfield, Stuart Henderson, John Herron, Simon Hill, Rupert Macnee,
Joe McIntyre, Gareth Owen, Jonathan Rigby, John Rodden, Mark Ward
and my editor Adam Newell.

The files at the British Film Institute were a valuable source of
contemporary quotes, and the following books provided similarly useful
information: *Armchair Theatre: The Lost Years* by Leonard White (Kelly
Publications, 2003), *The Avengers: The Inside Story* by Patrick Macnee
with Dave Rogers (Titan Books, 1997, 2008), *The Avengers On Location*
by Chris Bentley (Reynolds & Hearn, 2007) and *The Ultimate Avengers*
by Dave Rogers (Boxtree, 1995). In addition, I have also drawn upon the
interviews conducted by Paul Madden for his documentary *Without
Walls: The Avengers*, broadcast by Channel 4 on 14 January 1992.

The following websites proved to be reliable and exhaustive
reference works: *The Avengers Forever!* (www.theavengers.tv/forever),
edited by David K Smith, and *The Avengers Declassified*
(http://declassified.theavengers.tv/), edited by Alan Hayes.
Both are highly recommended.

Finally, my thanks to *The Avengers'* uncredited stills photographers,
whose pictures made this book possible.

Jacket front: A 1964 publicity still of Diana Rigg and Patrick Macnee, taken to
promote the fourth series of *The Avengers*.
Jacket back (top to bottom): Linda Thorson as Tara King in 'Whoever Shot
Poor George Oblique Stroke XR40?'; Diana Rigg as Mrs Emma Peel in
'The Town Of No Return'; Honor Blackman as Mrs Cathy Gale, wearing the
original green version of her leather fighting suit; Diana Rigg and Patrick
Macnee in a scene from the American pre-title sequence for Series Four.

Case front: Honor Blackman models the leather fighting suit designed by
Frederick Starke.
Case back: Linda Thorson in the Tara King episode 'All Done With Mirrors'.

Contents

Foreword

C an it really be 50 years since *The Avengers* began?

The series was conceived as a vehicle for a famous actor of the time, Ian Hendry. It was called *The Avengers* because we were avenging the death of Ian's character's fiancée, played by Catherine Woodville, who would eventually become my second wife.

The original series ran from 1961 to 1969. I was there on the first day, and I was there on the last. My son recently asked me what it was like to experience the 1960s. I said to him, "I never knew. I got into my car at five in the morning and got home at nine at night..."

We were a bunch of merry men and women, some of the finest craftsmen, creators and curators of a place that existed somewhere in our imaginations.

During early rehearsals the producers challenged me to make more of my character, John Steed. They said, "Patrick, can't you come up with something better?" I was very angry and stomped off, muttering under my breath, "Who the hell do they think they are?" I thought about my parents, my childhood, films from the 1930s and 40s, the war, my young family, my experiences in Canada and America as a struggling actor and the many and varied roles I had tackled. I turned around and said, "I've got it." I had the inspiration I needed.

Add black leather, a well-known fetish at the time, and blonde Honor Blackman in it, hurling evil men over her shoulder ... well. From then on we were a big success.

Honor was succeeded by the magnificent Diana Rigg, who helped to make *The Avengers* popular in America too. The series ended with Linda Thorson by my side; her youthful enthusiasm was infectious and revitalised the show once again. I could not have wished for three more beautiful and talented co-stars.

I understood, as I started reading the script for each new episode, that I would be given the key to a new world. Surrounding me was a host of writers, directors, set designers and actors, as well as wardrobe, sound, and lighting people, all with inspired shooting and editing skills. All were at the top of their game, at the right place, and at an extraordinary moment in time. What a privilege it was. What an amazing confluence of good luck, good timing and grace.

As I scan these pages of pictures, many of which I have never seen before, I am filled with pride at what we achieved.

I leave it to historians to figure out whether *The Avengers* 'mattered', to anthropologists, to experts of every kind. All I know is that we did it.

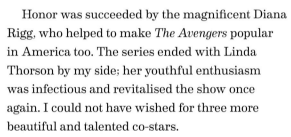

Patrick Macnee
Rancho Mirage
June 2010

Introduction

Below
Honor Blackman as Mrs Gale, waiting for her cue during the recording of 'The Golden Eggs' at Teddington Studios.

Opposite left
Diana Rigg as Mrs Peel, on the Elstree Studios set of the 'The House That Jack Built'.

THE AVENGERS WAS THE most stylish television series of its age. Even before the show was produced on film and sold around the world, an unusual emphasis was placed on the way it looked. "We were concerned with making what we called 'essential television'," says co-creator and original producer Leonard White. "We weren't copying theatre or cinema. We were creating something unique, with immediacy and personality."

Once the programme hit its stride, this personality was expressed in eccentric scripts, bold set designs and the creation of strong identities for the show's leads. The foundation of the series was Patrick Macnee as John Steed. Both he and his female partners were groomed and packaged in a way that both anticipated and encapsulated a new image-conscious era. Top photographer Terry O'Neill and supermodel Twiggy gladly joined the ranks of those associated with the programme when the 1960s began to swing.

The Avengers invested more than many other television programmes in quality still photography. This went beyond the portraits and scenes distributed to newspaper editors and extended to coverage of modelling sessions, *Avengers* fashion shows and lavish location shoots. Even the day-to-day unit photography is of an unusually high standard, and includes pictures that serve as a valuable record of early instalments that no longer exist. For the 1961 series there are numerous instances where boxes of still negatives are now all that survive from shows where tapes, film copies and even scripts are absent from the archive.

Fortunately the show's production company ABC Television preserved all the episodes from the second series onwards, and diligently maintained a near complete archive of still negatives, positives, transparencies and prints. This book is the result of an exhaustive survey of the estimated 10,000 images in the care of current rights-holders CANAL+. From these, more than 350 negatives

and prints were selected and scanned, before being subjected to several months of digital restoration.

The pictures serve as a record of one of the most successful television series ever produced in Britain, and a chronicle of a remarkable decade in fashion. At the programme's peak, even accessories such as hats, gloves and wristwatches were specially created in a mod *Avengers* style. Designers John Bates, Pierre Cardin, Harvey Gould, Alun Hughes, Frederick Starke and Michael Whittaker set the trends for the show, while Patrick Macnee designed many of his own suits. The wardrobe department at ABC followed in their wake, quietly contributing extraordinary ideas of their own.

The strength of the imagery in the stills suggests that the era was intrinsic to *The Avengers*' success. Many people involved in the show certainly consider that this worked against subsequent attempts to revive the format. "It's very closely associated with the 1960s," says director John Hough. "If you were to make a new series today you'd have to do it so differently from the way we made it that I don't think there'd be any point in calling it *The Avengers*."

Fellow director Roy Ward Baker, who did much to establish the most popular partnership of Patrick Macnee and Diana Rigg, considers that "It was of its time, and it ran out of time. I don't think audiences

become cynical about these things, but they do get bored. *The Avengers* ran its course."

Unless otherwise stated in captions, the evolution of that course is illustrated here by presenting the episodes in the order they were produced. This is a 50th anniversary celebration of the original show, and as such does not include chapters on its admirable 1970s sequel *The New Avengers*, the misjudged 1998 film, the stage play, radio series or any other spin-offs.

It's been said that the classic *Avengers* existed in a world of its own. It is that vibrant and enchanting parallel universe that we celebrate in the pages of this book.

Above
Linda Thorson as Tara King, relaxing on the set of John Steed's flat in the episode 'Split!'

Below left
One of the original press releases that have been preserved in the archive. These were collected with stills inside lavish folders, which were presented to journalists tied with ribbon.

Below
Another archive treasure: a box containing delicate glass negatives dating from 1962 to 1964.

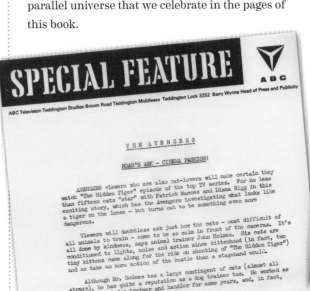

Series *One*

English Noir

IT IS IRONIC THAT *THE Avengers*, one of the 1960s' most sophisticated television series, evolved through a combination of necessity and accident.

It's similarly surprising that this quintessentially English show was initiated by a Canadian.

In 1958 Toronto-born Sydney Newman came to Britain to become the Head of Drama at the Associated British Corporation, better known as ABC Television. ABC had the ITV franchise to broadcast weekend television in the Midlands and the north of England, but also provided programmes that were screened across the entire network.

Newman was committed to social realism in ABC's dramatic output, and this was certainly evident in *Police Surgeon*, a series that presented 'True life dramas from a life few know'. Loosely combining the BBC's police drama *Dixon of Dock Green* with ATV's medical soap *Emergency – Ward 10* made for a promising format. ABC had made a similarly wise decision in casting the intense and charismatic Ian Hendry as the show's leading man.

Police Surgeon made its debut in September 1960, but behind-the-scenes problems had already condemned it to a run of just 13 episodes. Leonard White had only recently taken over as the show's producer when he learned it had been cancelled. "I was never told exactly why," he recalls. "Sydney said, 'We've got to stop *Police Surgeon*, but we need to keep Ian going – dream up another series for him.' We had to get the replacement show on the air in a matter of weeks."

White and story editors Patrick Brawn and John Bryce came up with characters for Ian Hendry and his co-star Ingrid Hafner that were very similar to the roles they had played in *Police Surgeon*. White proposed that the new series should be called *The Avengers*. "Sydney didn't know what it meant," he says. "He seemed to think it was something to do with revenge, and I pointed out that to *avenge* was to take action on behalf of somebody else. I said, 'It's sort of Robin Hood-ish,' and that rather tickled him."

Hendry would play Dr David Keel and Hafner was cast as his practice nurse Carol Wilson. The trio was completed by the shadowy and amoral intelligence agent John Steed, who involved them both in his investigations into the criminal underworld. "Ian was very believable, and he acted for the camera beautifully," says White. "His character was a working doctor and he had his feet on the ground. His counterpart was specially created for *The Avengers*; John Steed was the dilettante."

White suggested that Patrick Macnee, an actor he had shared a stage with in the 1950s, would be ideal for this enigmatic undercover man. "Patrick was the absolute essence of the English gentleman, but was getting known in Hollywood at the time. He happened to be in England in 1960 because he had produced a documentary on Winston Churchill for American television and was over here for some promotion. Sydney knew Patrick as well, so we decided to ask him to play Steed."

'Hot Snow', the first episode of *The Avengers*, was recorded 'as live' by its cast on 30 December 1960, less than a month after the broadcast of the final episode of *Police Surgeon*. The new series was first screened in the north on Saturday 7 January 1961. It wouldn't be seen in London until three months later.

Below
Dr Keel and Carol Wilson in a location shot taken to publicise 'The Frighteners', one of the few surviving episodes from the first series.

"We rehearsed in an old building opposite a pub in Hammersmith," Ian Hendry told the *TV Times* in 1976. "After the cast had been given their copies of the script, I would take them over to the pub, act as mine host, tell them not to worry because they were still on the payroll – and we'd get to work. Then Pat and myself, and sometimes a few others, would go to a nearby steak house. After that, it was usually Pat and I who would grab a bottle of scotch or brandy and go to a flat off Kensington High Street to beat out our latest approach to *The Avengers* characters."

The technical limitations of the era saddled the series with an unavoidably theatrical feel, but the cinematic influence of film noir was evident in the dark, inner city settings, the title sequence montage of Keel and Steed in crumpled raincoats and the sleazy incidental music. Crucially, however, even at this early stage everything from Johnny Dankworth's theme tune to John Steed's public school background received a distinctly English twist. Macnee would move Steed further away from the noir archetype by rarely using or even handling a gun, and taking sartorial inspiration from the dandyish spy Ralph Richardson had played in the 1939 film *Q Planes*.

In December 1961 the *TV Times* asked Ingrid Hafner to describe her co-stars. "[Ian] is intelligent and hard-working – and easily upset when things go wrong," she said. "But on the surface he's a great clown, not a bit like Keel. Pat is a more mature person than Ian in many ways. Unlike Steed, Pat has a quiet personality. He is controlled, modest and easy going ... Pat is a bit of a dreamer. He'll tell you this himself. I think he secretly wishes he was a character like Steed."

The show continued to evolve throughout 1961, although its progress must largely be deduced through photographs as only two complete episodes from the first series are known to survive. While Hendry and Macnee developed their characters' sometimes mistrustful relationship, the show's directors managed to forge a distinctive visual style within the confines of live studiobound production. Two of the early series' most distinctive directors were Don Leaver and Peter Hammond. "Peter loved to play with it," says White. "His shots were always exciting, but he was also able to decorate them in an

interesting way. Don Leaver was also excellent, but had a very different style. He was the realism man, in a sense."

"Peter had a filmic style, while a lot of the other directors at that time still had their feet in concrete," says Brian Clemens, who was part of the show's original writing team and scripted the second episode, 'Brought to Book'. "Peter realised that there was not much money available, and that it was silly to spend it on a huge set that you'd only see for three minutes. If you had a short scene set in a baker's he would put some loaves and a cake in the foreground and shoot through them. Suddenly you were in a baker's. So he was not only truncating the design but he was – subconsciously perhaps – introducing a style. And I think *The Avengers* was the first programme to have a definite shooting style. A lot of this came from Peter Hammond's imagery and Robert Fuest's set designs."

The first series was barely over when the actors' union Equity called a strike that prevented its members working for the ITV companies. "We breathed a sigh of relief in one respect, because it meant we could get ahead with our scripts," says White. "We couldn't predict that the strike would go for so long, however. By the time it was finally called off we had plenty of scripts in hand but Ian was no longer available because he'd got himself a nice fat film contract. It's been said that Ian left because he didn't want to continue with the series, but it wasn't like that at all. We were getting on very well."

Hendry left to launch his film career with a starring role in *Live Now – Pay Later*, and the departure of Dr Keel meant there was now no longer a role for Ingrid Hafner. Patrick Macnee elected to stay with *The Avengers*, and after the resolution of the strike found himself £5 a week better off.

The series would continue into 1962, but the producers would have to find a new lead to replace Ian Hendry. The character they chose would have a profound effect on British television.

Above
Director Peter Hammond, pictured here during rehearsals for the 1963 episode 'Warlock', did much to establish the series' distinctive visual style.

Below left
Steed visits Dr Keel's surgery in 'A Change of Bait'. The dangerous nature of Steed's schemes meant that Keel was a sometimes less-than-willing accomplice.

Below
A portrait of Patrick Macnee from 'Dead of Winter', the final episode of Series One.

← ← Hot Snow
Members of the production team are reflected in the jewellers' shop window as Ian Hendry and Catherine Woodville rehearse the first episode's fateful murder scene.

← Dance With Death
Interviewed by Paul Madden in *Screen First* magazine, Patrick Macnee described the influence of American film noir on the early episodes. "I think they cribbed it from New York, where they had *New York Confidential*," he said. "Everything was rugged clothes, two men in dirty macs going around looking macho and being buddies."

↙ The Springers
Location filming was extremely rare in the early series, but pictures from such sequences were frequently used to promote the show in newspapers and magazines.

↓ Death on the Slipway
"I'm enjoying this series because the makers are not afraid to inject humour into the episodes," Macnee told the *TV Times* in April 1961.

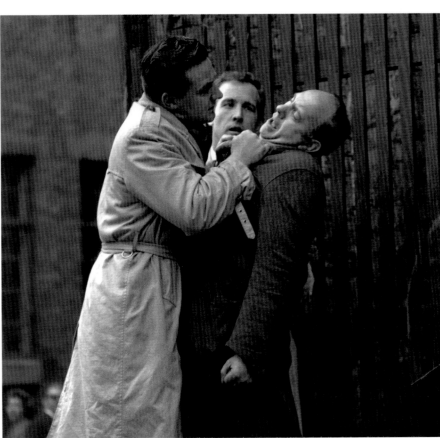

← Tunnel of Fear

'Straight from the Middle East – The Dance of Death.' A disguised Steed marshals a troupe of exotic girls at a Southend funfair. In December 1960 producer Leonard White had told the *TV Times*' Tim Aspinall, "The locations of the stories will be familiar to viewers but not familiar to them on television. We are doing everything to avoid clichés."

↘ Tunnel of Fear

Is that in the script? Patrick Macnee gets to the bottom of his new role. "The undercover man I play is a wolf with the women and revels in trouble," he told the *TV Times*.

↑ Tunnel of Fear
Inside the ghost train tunnel Maxie Lardner (Stanley Platts) hypnotises Steed in an effort to discover the purpose of his visit to Southend. Sinister funfair boss Jack Wickram (John Salew) waits for an answer.

→ Tunnel of Fear
Keel releases the captive Steed in time for the final confrontation with Wickram.

→→ Kill the King
In Studio 2 at Teddington, floor manager Patrick Kennedy rehearses guest artist Burt Kwouk for his role as King Tenuphon.

↑ **Kill the King**
King Tenuphon's bodyguard General Tuke
(Patrick Allen) admits to Steed that he is
a former deserter who never amounted to
more than an acting corporal in the
regular army.

➔ **The Deadly Air**
This was the highest-rated episode of the
first series, but only stills survive as a record
of the production. In this shot Steed and
Ken Armstrong (Anthony Cundell) discover
fragments of a glass phial in an air duct at
Truscott Research Laboratories.

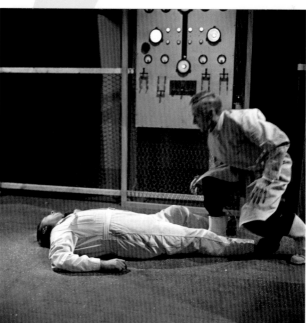

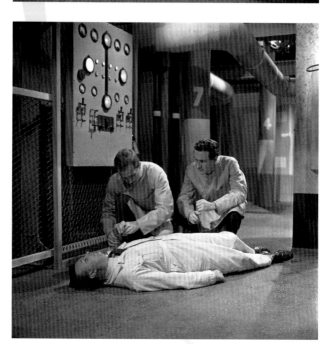

The Deadly Air
Heneager (Keith Anderson) is discovered by
Armstrong, and the two men grapple by the
ventilation controls. An injured Armstrong
stems the flow of poisoned air to the test
room and releases the door. Keel and Steed
arrive too late to save him.

→ The Deadly Air
Lester Powell's script for this episode made
good use of Dr Keel's medical expertise
during the investigation of sabotaged
vaccine tests. Ian Hendry had played a
doctor in *Police Surgeon* and was initially
wary of accepting such a similar role in
The Avengers. "Frankly, I thought twice
when asked to start out on another series
as a doctor," he told the *TV Times'* Tim
Aspinall in December 1960, "but as I know
the accent in the scripts is on authenticity, I
think it will do me a lot of good. And I know
it will be a lot of fun."

← **Dragonsfield**
The most intriguing of all the lost episodes from *The Avengers'* first series, *Dragonsfield* saw Steed embark on a solo mission in a space research centre. Staff at the centre have been deliberately exposed to deadly levels of radiation, and Steed suspects an inside job. In this picture the murderer, disguised in an anti-radiation suit, attacks laboratory assistant Lisa Strauss (Sylvia Langova).

↑ **Dragonsfield**
Barbara Shelley, cast as Susan Summers, clutches a copy of *The Daily Express* during rehearsals. Barbara would make another notable guest appearance in Series Five.

↗ **Dragonsfield**
Susan undresses in the shower room, and accuses Lisa of being obsessed with one of the scientists, Dr Redington.

→ **Dragonsfield**
The anti-radiation suit is retrieved from a stand on the laboratory set.

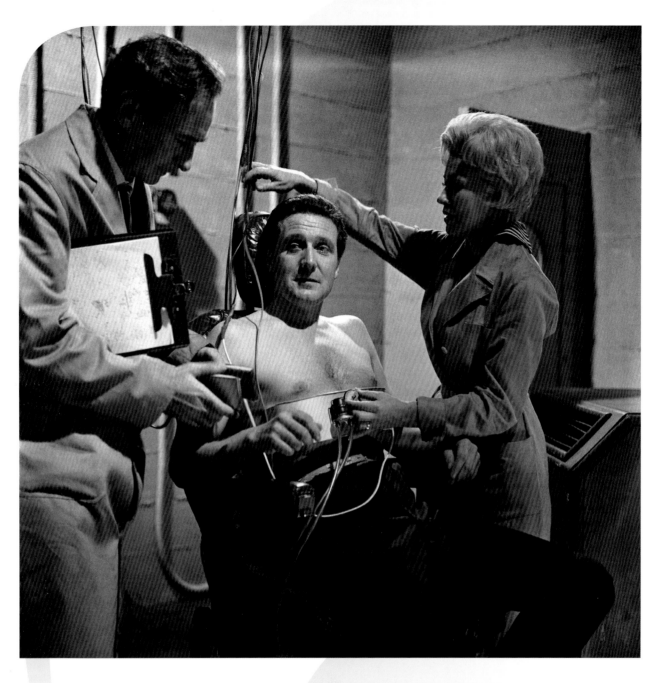

↑ Dragonsfield
Steed submits to a potentially dangerous
experiment that he hopes will flush the
saboteur out into the open. Dr Redington
(Ronald Leigh-Hunt) and Lisa Strauss attach
sensors that will monitor his vital signs.

→ Dragonsfield
Unfortunately the saboteur is one step ahead
of everyone – the machinery has already
been tampered with, and Steed endures an
agonising ordeal before he passes out.

→→ Dragonsfield
Ronald Leigh-Hunt catches up on some
reading during a break in rehearsals.

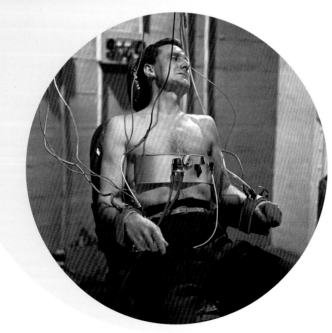

↑ **Dead of Winter**

"Let's say Steed is a slightly exaggerated version of myself," Patrick Macnee told the *TV Times'* Charles Bayne in May 1961. "Somebody once said to me: 'You should have lived in the 18th century.' I agree. Like Steed, I'm a great pretender. Anybody who loves the good life like I do has to be a pretender."

➔ **Dead of Winter**

Ian Hendry's final episode of *The Avengers* was recorded on 18 October 1961, and saw Keel in the clutches of the neo-Nazi organisation Phoenix. Their plan is to freeze their members in suspended animation, thus making them impervious to the effects of the nuclear war they are about to trigger.

↑ **Dead of Winter**

"For all experiments, one needs a guinea pig," says Dr Kreuzer (Arnold Marle). "I shall subject you to a controlled experiment lasting one month, during which you will be subjected to every known radiation hazard. Now relax, Dr Keel."

Series Two

Deadlier Than the Male

Opposite
Honor Blackman and Patrick Macnee outside the Teddington Studios' make-up room during production of 'The Mauritius Penny'.

Right
A September 1962 publicity shot taken on the set of 'Bullseye'. Patrick Macnee's style was already in place, even though Honor Blackman had yet to start wearing the leather outfits she would become renowned for.

Below
This sales brochure for the second series claimed *The Avengers'* appeal lay in its "off-beat twists and a strong vein of wacky humour, laced with an undercurrent of social conscience."

THE AVENGERS 2 AGAINST THE UNDERWORLD IN THIS EXCITING SERIES OF HOUR LONG PROGRAMMES FOR TELEVISION

THE AVENGERS BELATEDLY resumed recording in May 1962, seven months after the first series wrapped. Producer Leonard White and his story editor John Bryce had plenty of scripts in hand, but had still not decided on a permanent new partner for John Steed.

For the first three episodes of Series Two, Steed was joined by Dr Martin King, played by Jon Rollason. Substituting one doctor for another meant that the scripts didn't need much revision, but the results lacked the combative spark of Steed and Keel's relationship. Someone else had to be found, and discussions between Sydney Newman and Leonard White prompted an audacious proposal. "Sydney and I both wanted to see a woman in Ian Hendry's role," says White. "We wanted to see a woman playing the lead in a series, not a support. In those days this was very rare, if indeed it had ever happened at all."

Newman was inspired by the cultural anthropologist Margaret Mead, an outspoken American easily identified by her cape and forked walking stick. In 1985 he told Tim Collins that another strong female had also caught his eye. "At that time there was a lot of trouble in Kenya with the Mau Mau. I happened to see this newsreel

in which this 40 year-old matronly woman on a Kenyan settlers' farm was in the kitchen with a baby strapped to her back, and around her rather thickish waist was this great big revolver in a holster ... I looked at that woman with a gun on her hip and a baby on her back, telling about the death of her whole family. What a dame, I thought! I remember in my memorandum describing this newsreel I'd seen and I said we should turn [Ian Hendry's character] into a woman but make sure the chemistry was exactly the same – she should disapprove of Patrick Macnee and she should be adept physically."

The new *Avengers* lady would be Mrs Cathy Gale, a tough anthropologist whose husband had been murdered on their farm in Africa. White consulted Peter Hammond and Don Leaver over casting and presented Newman with a list of potential Cathys that had Honor Blackman at the top and Nyree Dawn Porter at the bottom. Newman had a clear preference for Porter, so transposed the two names and left to go on holiday, confident that discussions would continue or that Porter would have been cast by the time he returned.

White had other ideas. "Both of them worked for me, but – and I don't mean this at all unkindly – Dawn was from New Zealand and there was something about her that didn't seem to be

Series Two

sufficiently English for the role of Mrs Gale." Much to Newman's eventual surprise, White went with his original choice.

"They got Honor Blackman, who was a beautiful blonde with a bosom to take your breath away, the hips of a boy scout and long, runners' legs," says Patrick Macnee. "They didn't alter the scripts at all, which were written for a man, so she thought, I'll play it as if I'm stronger than a man. Which indeed she was."

John Bryce found it surprisingly simple to adapt the remaining Dr Keel scripts for Mrs Gale, and the slightly uneasy dynamic that had existed between Steed and Keel was preserved. "Cathy and Steed were pretty equal," says Honor Blackman. "They differed insofar as his thinking was more devious than hers. She was a much more upright character, and never played dirty."

Alongside Dr King and Mrs Gale, the second series featured another partner for Steed – the largely forgotten Venus Smith, who appeared in six episodes. "We created Dr King and Venus to try to relieve the pressure on the two main leads in terms of scripting," says White. "Venus was

created as an entirely different character from Cathy Gale. Her character could take the stories into underworld settings where Keel and Cathy Gale wouldn't necessarily have belonged."

Julie Stevens had been a contract artist at ABC for five years when she was abruptly dropped by managing director Howard Thomas in August 1962. "I received a letter from Howard suggesting that I should now settle down and have children," she recalls, laughing. "And then a few days later, on a Friday morning, I got a phone call from my agent saying they wanted me for *The Avengers*. So I went along and met the director, Don Leaver, and Leonard White. Don said 'I don't think she can do it,' and Leonard said, 'I think she can.' I went home and that evening got a phone call asking if I could come back and sing. So I got on the bus back to Teddington Studios and met a lovely jazz pianist called Dave Lee. I was fully aware I couldn't swing, but Dave said, 'Leave it to us – we'll do the swinging.' I sang a couple of numbers with Dave and went home again. At ten o'clock they called me again and asked if I could be at rehearsals the following morning. It turns

Below
The Avengers' first three series were made at ABC Television's Teddington Studios. This still shows how the studio floor was sub-divided for the recording of 'Death of a Great Dane' in October 1962.

Below right
"The clothes were slightly tailored and the numbers were classics," recalls Julie Stevens of the cabaret sequences in her first two episodes. "I didn't mind that, but they put me in this rather staid blonde wig that made me look older than my years."

out they'd actually started rehearsing even though they didn't have a Venus. Negotiations continued after that and they paid me £200 an episode. Of course if they'd got me while I was still under contract they could have had me for £35 a week."

Julie had worked on numerous live productions at Teddington, and making *The Avengers* was similarly nerve-racking. Each episode was recorded in one long take, stopping only for filmed inserts and commercial breaks. "During rehearsals Patrick was running up and down the stairs doing two episodes at once," she says, "and when we came to do the actual episode it was even more frantic. You'd walk through a door saying, 'See you tomorrow,' and then come back through a different door in a different outfit five seconds later. It was an adrenaline rush. As soon as you heard the ABC jingle and the Johnny Dankworth theme there was no way back."

In December 1962 Sydney Newman defected to the BBC where, among other things, he would launch *Doctor Who* and *The Wednesday Play*. He asked Leonard White to go with him, but White instead chose to stay at ABC and take over *Armchair Theatre*, which he produced until 1969. Story editor John Bryce was promoted and took over as the producer of *The Avengers*. "Leonard loved *Armchair Theatre* passionately so I could understand why he went, but we were sorry to see him go," says Honor Blackman. "John Bryce was great though. He was a bit younger and was more 'mod' in his outlook."

Bryce decided to radically alter Venus' character and gave Julie Stevens a more up-to-date look. "When the script for my third episode came she suddenly seemed completely different,

a bit Northern and slightly kooky," says Julie. "I didn't have any control over it at all."

By the end of the second series Dr King was a distant memory and Bryce decided to drop Venus Smith as well. "I wasn't surprised they let me go because I had no confidence in myself, and Honor was just so fantastic," says Julie. "I only found out later that Leonard would have kept me on if he had stayed."

However, Bryce was keen to further explore the pairing of John Steed and Cathy Gale – urbane agent and tough female amateur. *The Avengers* had finally found a durable new format.

Above left
Honor Blackman's Cathy Gale emerged as the most popular of Steed's three partners during the second series.

Above
You're nicked! WPC Mary Williams puts Patrick Macnee in an armlock during his visit to a Halifax police station on 29 August 1962.

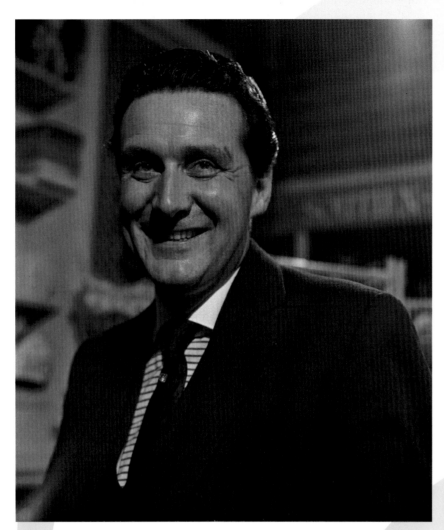

✈ Mission to Montreal

When *The Avengers* returned for its second
series Dr Keel was gone. An ABC Television
press release prepared viewers for a revolving
door of sidekicks, and profiled the actor who
was now the star of the show: "Patrick Macnee's
television character parallels his own liking for
elegant clothes, good food, wine, fast cars and
pretty girls."

✈ Mission to Montreal

The first three stories into production partnered
Steed with Dr Martin King, played by Jon
Rollason. It was no coincidence that King and
Keel seemed so alike – the scripts had been
written with Ian Hendry in mind and received
little updating for the new actor.

✈ Mission to Montreal

Australian actress Pamela Ann Davy only had
a small role in this episode, but joined Patrick
Macnee for a publicity shoot in which she
modelled some gear that was pretty way-out by
the standards of the day. Pamela later auditioned
for the role of Venus Smith, appeared in the 1967
episode 'The Living Dead', and was reportedly a
leading contender to play Tara King.

✈✈ Mission to Montreal

Disguised as a ship's steward, Steed uses the
pretence of room service to rendezvous with Dr
King. "Free trip on a luxury liner, sea air, only
one patient, it's marvellous," says the doctor.

Inevitably Steed has to point out that, "It's not
quite as simple as that..."

← Dead on Course

In the highest-rated episode of the second series, Freedman (John McLaren) and Steed take the controls of a transatlantic flight they suspect is about to be sabotaged. Air stewardess Deirdre (Elisabeth Murray) and passenger Vincent (Donal Donnelly) have good reason to look anxious.

↑ Dead on Course

Steed and Dr King investigate two air crashes in the same remote area of Ireland, and the subsequent theft of the planes' valuable cargo. The only survivor of the latest crash is murdered while in the care of nuns, but the strangely impassive Mother Superior (Peggy Marshall) refuses to let Steed search her convent.

→ Dead on Course

As Steed's plane is misdirected on a collision course he strangles a confession from Vincent, who reveals the location of the stolen money.

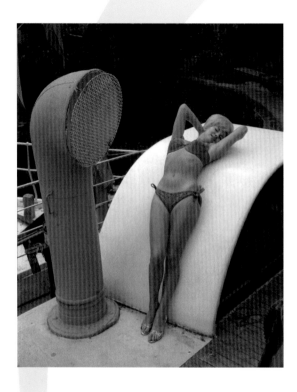

↑ **Death Dispatch**
In June 1962 Caron Gardner, one of this episode's uncredited bikini girls, sunbathes on a boat moored at the back of Teddington Studios.

↗ **Death Dispatch**
Tourist attraction: in Jamaica, Steed's roving eye spots a potential new friend by the hotel pool.

→ **Death Dispatch**
Honor Blackman rehearses the scene where she waits for Steed to arrive at her hotel room. "Are you decent?" he asks her on the phone. "I shall be by the time you get here," she replies.

→→ **Death Dispatch**
In Mrs Gale's bedroom Steed offers his new partner a "livener" before they leave for Santiago. "Thanks," she says, "even if there are strings attached."

← Mr Teddy Bear

Mrs Gale is to hire the professional assassin Mr Teddy Bear to kill Steed. In the back room of a photographic shop Steed prepares the ruse by playing a tape-recording of the man Cathy will claim is her superior.

↑ Mr Teddy Bear

An amused Steed reveals that the fingerprints Mrs Gale retrieved from her bizarre encounter with Mr Teddy Bear appear to belong to an adult chimpanzee!

↗ Mr Teddy Bear

Seen as very much a prototype for the more outlandish episodes that would follow, 'Mr Teddy Bear' was recorded sixth in the schedule but shown first when *The Avengers* returned to screens in September 1962. This decision meant that viewers received a rather abrupt introduction to Mrs Cathy Gale, with few initial clues about the character's background. Her expertise in judo was, however, made clear in this scene set in Steed's flat.

→ The Decapod

Steed grapples with a masked murderer, but is this the wrestler known as the Decapod or an imposter?

← Bullseye

Patrick Macnee makes a point while rehearsing with Honor Blackman. The London Stock Exchange was represented by sparse set decoration, but director Peter Hammond skilfully disguised the shortcomings with tight camera shots and foreground activity.

↑ Bullseye

Soldiers from the Coldstream Guards show Honor Blackman how to handle a rifle for the scenes set in the butts of Anderson's Small Arms.

↗ Bullseye

Honor Blackman is made up for the closing scenes. Her leather fighting suit earned designer Michael Whittaker a 'Special Wardrobe' credit at the end of this episode.

← Warlock

Honor Blackman and Patrick Macnee join choreographer Pat Kirshner's rehearsals for the black magic ceremony at the climax of this episode. Originally recorded in July 1962, 'Warlock' drew upon Mrs Gale's expert knowledge of voodoo and was conceived as her introductory episode. When 'Mr Teddy Bear' was moved forward in the schedule, certain scenes in 'Warlock' were remounted so as not to appear incongruous.

↑ Box of Tricks

Julie Stevens is backed by The Dave Lee Trio for one of Venus' cabaret numbers. Directly behind her is double bassist Spike Heatley. The two were reunited in the 1970s when Julie became one of the presenters of the BBC children's programme *Play Away* and Spike was a member of the house band.

→ Box of Tricks

"When John Bryce became the producer I was sent to Vidal Sassoon in Bond Street to have my hair cut," remembers Julie. "He got rid of my curls and gave me this hairdo which was ahead of its time, because six months later the Beatles cut became trendy."

← The Golden Eggs
Mrs Gale moves some of her belongings, and a delicate restoration project, into Steed's Westminster Mews flat.

↑ The Golden Eggs
Patrick Macnee and Honor Blackman get a dusting of fake snow on this episode's scrapyard set.

→ The Golden Eggs
This publicity picture was taken on the set of Steed's flat and subsequently used as the cover shot of the 1963 souvenir magazine *Meet the Avengers*, 'An exciting behind the scenes visit with the stars of ABC's top TV show'.

← Conspiracy of Silence

Honor Blackman had only recently married actor Maurice Kaufmann when she started work on *The Avengers*, but this didn't stop Patrick Macnee making a pass at her after a rehearsal. In his autobiography *Blind In One Ear* he recalled her response. "Oh, Patrick, come off it," she told him. "This is neither the time nor the place. I'm sweating like hell, my feet are killing me, I smell like a polecat and the answer's 'No'."

↑ School for Traitors

Venus and Steed adopted a casual look for this episode. Venus' blue-and-green sweater was from Jaeger. Steed's five-button sports jacket was inspired by a Hardy Amies design and tailored for Macnee by Hepworth. The menswear chain shed its dowdy image in the 1980s and is now better known as Next.

→ Killer Whale

"I am glad that [Steed's] Edwardian clothes with their braided pin-stripe suits, embroidered waistcoats, cummerbunds and curly bowlers are helping to set a new fashion for men," wrote Patrick Macnee in *Meet the Avengers*. "I find them elegant and pleasing to wear and feel they do a great deal to restore the male's masculine attraction."

Series Three

The Total Image

Left

A publicity shot – unusually showing Patrick Macnee holding a gun – taken on the set of 'Death of a Batman' in August 1963. The studio floor is covered in anticipation of an impending rain shower.

Right

Patrick Macnee and Honor Blackman rehearse 'Kinky Boots' and its flipside 'Let's Keep It Friendly' in February 1964. The record was not a hit until 26 years later.

Below

The first *Avengers* fashion show was held on 29 October 1963. Patrick Macnee wore clothes designed by Hardy Amies, and Honor Blackman modelled a collection by Frederick Starke.

HE THIRD SERIES OF *The Avengers* was recorded from April 1963 to March 1964, a tumultuous era that witnessed the first female Cosmonaut, the emergence of America's black civil rights movement and the assassination of President Kennedy. In England, the Profumo scandal and the arrival of Beatlemania suggested that the old order was stumbling in the face of a vibrant and influential new youth culture.

This collision of old and new was symbolised by the exaggerated stylings of *The Avengers*. Steed may have dressed like an establishment figure in a pin-stripe suit, bowler hat and brolly, but he was no square. He could be callous and occasionally sexist, but his unswerving dedication to British justice set him apart from the corrupt politicians and traitorous spies making the headlines in the early 1960s.

The arrival of Cathy Gale could have been perfectly timed to make her a figurehead for the burgeoning Women's Lib movement, but John Steed and Mrs Gale enjoyed a productive and platonic relationship. In their world, sex was no longer as important as getting the job done.

These increasingly outlandish characters and their unique relationship only fuelled criticisms that the show was now divorced from reality. In the 1963 souvenir magazine *Meet the Avengers*, story editor Richard Bates proudly defended the third series' capacity to surprise its audience. "I wanted [the stories] to be exciting but fun, unusual but comprehensible, different but still adventurous," he said. "Nothing could be too good, every episode had to be about something new and presented in an exciting way. I think on most occasions we succeeded, and the final credit for the high standard of this present series must go to the scriptwriters."

These writers now once again included Brian Clemens, who had last contributed to Series One. "I think television is a writers' medium; if you haven't got good writers you haven't got a good show," he says. "And for that reason I think *The Avengers* was run by its story editors. I got on well with Richard from day one. We shared the same sense of humour. He allowed and encouraged me to take the show in an increasingly surreal direction."

Honor Blackman had brought her own ideas to the fore when she suggested that Mrs Gale should be a judo expert, rather than defending herself by scrabbling inside her handbag for a gun. "I loved *The Avengers* but there was so much physicality in it for me and it was hellish hard work," she says. "Patrick always used to worry like mad about the fight scenes. He used to say, 'Why don't you fight like me with an umbrella or a sword?' But the

Series Three

whole point of *The Avengers* was that she was the
sort of butch character and he was her cunning
companion. Never mind the fights, to get Steed to
even run anywhere was quite something.

"We did an episode every two weeks, and I had
to find time to learn my lines, rehearse my fights
and go to the gym. I learned my judo all out of
time. I should have started with simple throws
and then graduated, but they kept giving me
stomach throws because it's about the only judo
throw that looks dramatic."

Patrick Macnee made a suggestion of his own
when he proposed that Honor Blackman should
have more practical attire for her fight scenes.
Michael Whittaker had designed four basic outfits
for Mrs Gale in Series Two, anticipating the
vogue for man-tailored style and high boots. For
Series Three, Cathy's wardrobe would change to
encompass increasing amounts of leather. "I don't
know why, but my leather suits were green to
start out with," remembers Honor. "The episodes

weren't in colour so I suppose it didn't make that
much difference, but it was much more sexy to
change to black."

Following a variety of prototypes, Mrs Gale's
ultimate black leather fighting suit made its
debut in the episode 'November Five'. The first
time Patrick Macnee saw Honor wearing it he
was so captivated that he forgot his lines. The
suit was created by London couturier Frederick
Starke, who also designed Honor's clothes for 14
additional episodes. Starke's designs made an
enormous impact on viewers, and helped Honor
to get into character. "In my fighting leather I
know I'm someone who can meet anyone, man or
woman, on equal terms," she wrote in *The Daily
Mail* on 22 January 1964. "Cathy is a complex
creation, with all kinds of taboos hedging her
round. She cannot be seen brushing her teeth.
She must not be touched by a man. She cannot be
seen to have a lover. All these things go into the
creation of the total image."

Starke's design was so successful that plans were made to market a range of leather fighting suits in the same style. Unfortunately no-one thought to tell Honor Blackman. "One day I went for a fitting with Frederick, and I found yards and yards of these leather suits all hanging up," she says. "I asked him why there were so many and he told me they were selling them. I thought it would have been nice to have been asked about this. Anyway, they didn't sell them!"

One spin-off that she was happy to take part in was the novelty tune 'Kinky Boots', which she and Patrick Macnee recorded for Decca in February 1964. This mercifully brief effort failed to dent the Hit Parade at the time, but went top five in 1990 following its rediscovery by Radio 1 DJ Simon Mayo.

By 1964 plans were in place to move the series to the Elstree Studios owned by ABC's previously remote parent organisation, the Associated British Picture Corporation. The next series of *The Avengers* would be shot on film, but Honor Blackman wouldn't be going with it. She decided to leave when the show's popularity, and her own profile, were at a peak. Like Ian Hendry, she had been offered a film contract (in her case a starring role as Pussy Galore in *Goldfinger*) and had found it impossible to resist. "Patrick was very upset when I told him, and there was a period when he didn't really talk to me," she admits. "We'd been together for two years and I decided right at the beginning that two years would be long enough. They must have realised that my contract was coming to an end, but I don't think anybody really expected me to go. A lot of people cried 'traitor' and that was a pity, but the excitement of this business is never knowing what's around the corner. I'm not one of those people who can go on year after year without that excitement."

As production wound down at Teddington Studios, John Bryce was visited by television critic L Marsland Garner. In the 9 March edition of *The Daily Telegraph*, Garner described their meeting.

"Mr Bryce calls the series 'surrealist', and says that it became the sort of parody that it is on his initiative, and that of the writers. They were not pushed into it by the ratings or public reaction."

Earlier that year, the *New Statesman*'s Francis Hope had already identified an increasingly bizarre trend in the show's storytelling. On 31 January 1964 he wrote, "Plots may offer opportunities for reaching out and making contact, sentimentally or realistically, with the outside world, but style forbids it."

The Avengers had already outgrown the influence of its creators. Under the control of new producers it would evolve once again.

Opposite right
The Variety Club named Patrick Macnee and Honor Blackman ITV Personalities of the Year, and on 19 March 1964 Harold Wilson presented them with their silver hearts. Honor had recorded her final episode of *The Avengers* the day before.

Left
Shortly after the third series ended, Patrick Macnee joined Fenella Fielding in an episode of the television series *Love Story*. 'Divorce, Divorce' was broadcast on 19 May 1964.

Below
Patrick Macnee strides along Broom Road, the home of Teddington Studios. *The Avengers* would relocate to Elstree in October 1964.

← **Brief for Murder**

Honor Blackman sets sail for a filmed location sequence. Such excursions were rare in the videotaped series. "Even then we didn't go far," says the story's author, Brian Clemens. "That looks like the studio's back garden!"

↑ **Brief for Murder**

Steed 'assassinates' Mrs Gale and Honor Blackman swaps places with her stunt double. "I'm not a great swimmer, so somebody else fell in for me," remembers Honor. She still had to get wet in order to be filmed emerging from the river, but this part of the sequence was ultimately dropped from the programme.

↗ **The Nutshell**

Guest star Edina Ronay, daughter of food critic Egon Ronay and subsequently a noted fashion designer, poses for a publicity shot inside an escapologist's sack.

↑ Death à la Carte

Steed assumes the guise of Sebastian Stone-Martin, chef des viandes, in order to prevent the murder of hotel guest Emir Abdulla Akaba. An ornate cake tray provides a vital clue, but Steed suspects that Josie (Coral Atkins) may have polished away the evidence.

→ The Grandeur That Was Rome

"Patrick Macnee, bouncing through his lines with umbrella, bowler hat and after-shave lotion smugness stretching from ear to ear, is a true musical-comedy mixture of caricature and sheer fantasy," wrote Francis Hope in the *New Statesman* in January 1964. "His absurdity saves us from too close an identification with his exploits (nobody could want to be *like* Steed) without diminishing their impact."

← The Grandeur That Was Rome

Steed is caught red-handed by 'Appolodorus' Eastow (Ian Shand), the public relations officer of United Foods and Dressings. *The Avengers* was becoming increasingly outlandish – in this episode the villain models his organisation on the Roman Empire – but producer John Bryce was determined that the series should maintain its credibility. Bryce was disappointed with 'The Grandeur That Was Rome', and circulated a memo that insisted, "We have got to see Steed get out of his predicament, or explain, convincingly, how he does so ... We have got to be at the very least supplied with, if not utterly convinced by, the denouement."

↑ The Undertakers

Story editor Richard Bates (left) with writers Malcolm Hulke (centre) and Brian Clemens. Bates recalls that his greatest challenge was to find suitable scripts for this unique series. "I interviewed 80 writers," he says. "I think I commissioned 30, and we ended up employing about five or six."

↑ Build a Better Mousetrap
Patrick Macnee joins Honor Blackman on
the back of her Royal Enfield during a night
shoot in Cobham Common. Honor had
learned to ride a motorcycle during the war,
while working for the civil service. "I soon
got the hang of it again and it was quite a
thrill," she told the *TV Times*.

→ Build a Better Mousetrap
Honor Blackman was more than capable
of handling all her own scenes in this
episode, but her 'Brief for Murder' stunt
double came along to ride another bike
during the filming of the ton-up gang.

↘↘ November Five
Michael Dyter has been elected to
Parliament for just one-and-a-half seconds
before he is assassinated. Steed investigates
the murder at the offices of Dyter's publicity
consultant, Mark St John.

← **November Five**

Mrs Gale apprehends Fiona (Iris Russell) at the Slimarama Sports Centre. Honor Blackman is wearing a leather fighting suit designed by Frederick Starke.

↑ **November Five**

"What would you say to standing for Parliament?" Steed asks Mrs Gale in this episode. "I'd vote for you."

↗ **November Five**

Steed explains why the House of Commons was chosen as the detonating point for a stolen nuclear warhead. "Guy Fawkes himself couldn't have wished for more."

→ **November Five**

"Couldn't I write my own clichés?" asks Mrs Gale as she listens to the speech Steed has drafted for her campaign.

← **The Gilded Cage**
Director Bill Bain trains his cameras low
to record the exchange between Mrs Gale
and her wardress (Margo Cunningham) at
Holloway Prison.

↑ **Dressed to Kill**
Strangeness on a train: Steed attends a
New Year's Eve fancy dress party held in a
railway carriage. "Don't you think it's just
fabby?" says 'Pussy Cat' (Anneke Wills).

→ **Dressed to Kill**
The party grinds to a halt at Badger's
Mount. Steed has an ally in Mrs Gale, who
gatecrashes wearing the highwaywoman's
discarded costume.

↑ Dressed to Kill
Patrick Macnee and John Junkin pose for a
publicity still in anticipation of the episode's
Wild West shoot-out.

→ The Wringer
Lovell (Gerald Sim), a department
operative working undercover as a tailor,
provides Steed with information about the
whereabouts of a fellow agent. Sim was
one of *The Avengers'* most prolific guest
artists, playing five different roles in the
original series.

→→ Mandrake
"Perhaps the most intriguing aspect of
Cathy Gale is her relationship with Steed,"
Honor Blackman told *The Daily Mail* in
January 1964. "Steed and Cathy Gale are *not*
lovers. They are close, working friends. I see
Pat every day, and our friendship is more
successful than it could possibly be if we
were having a love affair in private life."

← Mandrake

The increasing complexity of Mrs Gale's fight scenes prompted the decision to pre-record many of them the day before the taping of their respective episodes. On 15 January 1964 Honor Blackman and wrestler Jackie Pallo performed a carefully choreographed fight alongside an open grave at Teddington Studios. "Things had been going wrong over and over again," Blackman told *The Daily Mail* the day after. "We'd shot part of the scene a number of times and Jackie had twice cracked his head against the grave's headstone. There was blood about where I'd put my boot in his face too hard. Then he did this dive over a hedge, ending with a three foot drop into the grave. He landed smack on his head."

Pallo was unconscious for seven-and-a-half minutes, while a distraught Blackman sobbed by the side of the grave. She anxiously accompanied him back to his dressing room, where he eventually recovered. "I was fighting her for a shovel," he explained to *The Daily Sketch*. "She let go, and I fell into the grave. I want it to be made perfectly clear that this was an accident. I have never been beaten by a woman, and never intend to be. She was supposed to win in the end, but definitely not in this way."

↓ The Charmers

Steed takes part in an agent exchange scheme and is passed off with desperate actress Kim Lawrence (Fenella Fielding). Much confusion ensues during a visit to a gents' outfitters.

→ The Charmers

Mrs Gale cuts a dash at the Academy of Charm for Aspiring Young Gentlemen. This was one of the final episodes of Series Three, and Honor Blackman had already decided to leave the show.

She recorded her last episode, 'Lobster Quadrille', on 20 March 1964. The script included a sly reference by Steed to her forthcoming portrayal of Pussy Galore in *Goldfinger*.

Honor left *The Avengers* with her "only happy memories" and a pair of Cathy's leather boots which she still keeps as a souvenir.

Series Four
Extraordinary Crimes

THE AVENGERS THAT modern audiences know and love began production at the end of 1964. Patrick Macnee remained steadfast in the role of John Steed, but in many other respects Series Four was a radically different programme. Produced at Elstree Studios by Julian Wintle, the show was now made on 35mm film and aimed at an international market.

Such a move had previously been opposed by ABC's Head of Studio Bernard Greenhead, who feared it would put the production at the mercy of unions who had already disrupted the BBC's efforts to make filmed drama series. In 1964, however, ABC made the necessary investment to take a calculated risk on *The Avengers*. They committed to produce an initial 13 episodes on film in an effort to sell the show to an American television network.

Wintle enlisted Albert Fennell and Brian Clemens as his associate producers. "They wanted someone who knew *The Avengers* and also knew about film and I was uniquely qualified," says Clemens. "Albert came from big movies so he managed the unit and took care of all the day-to-day problems. He also took the dominant role in post-production. Apart from that the creativity was left to me."

Clemens had already hinted that Steed was about to recruit someone new in the closing scene of Honor Blackman's final episode, 'Lobster Quadrille', although we wouldn't get to see her until the following year. Steed's latest female partner was developed by Clemens along very similar lines as Mrs Gale, but she was named Mrs Emma Peel by ABC's press officer Marie Donaldson, who was amused by the pun on 'M appeal', ie 'man appeal'.

Wintle cast Elizabeth Shepherd in the role without a screen test, but she only made the first episode, 'The Town Of No Return', and half of its follow-up, 'The Murder Market', before she was released from her contract. "We saw the rushes and she wasn't giving us anything," says Clemens. "She was a competent actress but not an *Avengers* girl. Stopping production cost money, but we felt we had to recast and this time we tested."

The successful applicant was the Royal Shakespeare Company's Diana Rigg. She had impressed ABC's Howard Thomas with her recent performance in 'The Hothouse', an instalment of *Armchair Theatre* produced by Leonard White. "We tested her along with ten or 12 other actresses and she came out head and shoulders above the rest," says Clemens. "She was obviously new, young and vibrant. We only had

Opposite
After a false start with another actress, the role of Emma Peel went to Diana Rigg. In this August 1965 picture Diana models 'Flash', the John Bates-designed outfit she wore in the episode 'Castle De'ath'.

Right
This 1966 flyer was used to market the new filmed series of *The Avengers* around the world.

Below
Patrick Macnee and Diana Rigg celebrate the sale of *The Avengers* to America's ABC network at a champagne reception in 1965.

A Series of 26 ONE HOUR PROGRAMMES for TELEVISION

WATCH OUT FOR THE AVENGERS

starring:
PATRICK MACNEE as JOHN STEED
DIANA RIGG as EMMA PEEL

to wait while they tailored clothes for her and we were away."

Production continued with a remount of 'The Murder Market'. Later in the schedule director Roy Ward Baker (at that time credited as Roy Baker) remade 'The Town Of No Return', substituting Elizabeth Shepherd's scenes with new footage of Diana Rigg. Baker had been invited to join the series by Julian Wintle, who had produced his 1957 film *The One That Got Away* and had more recently asked him to contribute to his filmed television series *The Human Jungle*. Along with Charles Crichton, Sidney Hayers, James Hill and other feature film veterans, Baker was part of a new team that brought fresh production values to the series. Only two directors – Don Leaver and Bill Bain – were retained from the show's videotape days.

"It was intriguing and interesting right from the word go," says Baker. "*The Avengers* really suited me down to the ground, and I think perhaps I suited it. The series had wit, which is very rare on television. You get belly laughs on television, but you very rarely get wit. It was a sophisticated show and it was quite permissible to include jokes, or to play some of the existing lines as jokes, without reference to the producers. We felt that the audience had to catch up with us – we weren't going to condescend to them. This was something that many of us had longed to do. We felt it was high time television grew up."

Baker was impressed by Albert Fennell, whom he describes as "a devoted worker, who spent long hours in the studio long after everyone else had gone home. He was especially good at assessing the editing of a picture as it was coming together. I saw much less of Brian when we were making the show because he was working on the scripts, but he deserves tremendous credit for these episodes of *The Avengers*. He guided all the other writers and his influence was there on the screen."

Another new member of the team was composer Laurie Johnson, whose *Avengers* theme and incidental music embodied the playful, effervescent spirit of the filmed episodes. "Laurie was an asset and the score was brilliant," says Baker. "It was modern, it was jazzy, it was big and it was lush."

Above

Patrick Macnee outside Elstree Studios during production of 'The Cybernauts' in March 1965.

Below

Pictures from the pre-title sequence specially filmed to introduce American audiences to *The Avengers*.

Clemens' *Avengers* slightly softened the character of Steed and introduced a warmer rapport between him and his new partner. Clemens and his fellow scriptwriters – notably Philip Levene, Roger Marshall and Tony Williamson – delighted in experimenting with genres and danced a fine line between comedy and suspense. "There is a strong element of science-fiction in the new stories, including robots and a man-eating plant," promised one of Marie Donaldson's press releases. "But the whole thriller format is sent up even more openly and deliberately than in those early *Avenger* days before the Bond films and *The Man from UNCLE* consolidated the trend set by ABC's programme."

Key to the new series' success was Diana Rigg, both kittenish and capable as the self-assured Emma Peel. "Diana was an absolute gift," says Roy Ward Baker. "She hadn't done much television before – she was and ever shall be a theatre lady – but she was unbelievably professional and always word-perfect. She wasn't egotistical, but she did know her own value. One day I asked her why she was doing *The Avengers*, and she said, 'To make me famous.' Which it did, of course. She was a superior actress with a superior mind."

An impressive wardrobe was created for Diana by John Bates of the Jean Varon label, and while

she had her own version of the leather fighting suit she was also one of the first actresses to appear on screen wearing a mini-skirt. The American network ABC (no connection to the British *Avengers* producer) was impressed with the new package and ordered a full season of 26 episodes.

Anxious to introduce the series to an unfamiliar audience, the ABC network commissioned their own pre-title sequence. "Extraordinary crimes against the people and the state have to be avenged by agents extraordinary," declared the voice-over, as Steed and Mrs Peel retrieved a bottle of champagne from a corpse on a giant chess board. "Two such people are John Steed, top professional, and his partner Emma Peel, talented amateur ... otherwise known as the Avengers."

The programme was now a hit on both sides of the Atlantic. The next logical step was to film its fifth series in colour.

Left
In February 1966 bandleader Joe Loss visited Diana Rigg and Patrick Macnee at Elstree to promote his version of the *Avengers* theme, which was backed with a cover of the theme from *Thunderbirds*. "Although I've listened to the music from many shows over the past two years, I haven't found anything as exhilarating as *The Avengers* and *Thunderbirds*," he said.

Below
Diana Rigg models 'VIP' (left) and 'Blackboard', two more outfits designed by John Bates for the fourth series. Every item in the collection was available to buy, from Kangol's 'Avenger' beret to the Reginald Bernstein suits and Rayne boots.

The Town Of No Return

Filming of the fourth series began with the original version of 'The Town Of No Return', directed by Peter Graham Scott. Elizabeth Shepherd played Mrs Emma Peel, and is seen here on location at RAF Bircham Newton (opposite) and Holkham National Nature Reserve. Her distinctive hooded outfit was by renowned American designer Bonnie Cashin.

← Dial a Deadly Number
Patrick Macnee and Diana Rigg are dressed for Henry Boardman's dinner party in this publicity still. Mrs Peel's style was evolving, and this is one of several fur coats that Diana wore in her earliest episodes.

↑ The Murder Market
"Last night's sinister frolics in a marriage bureau were riveting in their precise and prolific fantasy," wrote Mary Crozier in *The Guardian* of 13 November 1965. "Emma nearly got herself buried alive – what a penchant these programmes have for burials and graveyard scenes!"

→ The Murder Market
"Fabulous!" *The Avengers* heralds the Swinging Sixties in this scene, where a photographer (John Forgeham) is bowled over by Steed's fashion tip.

↑ Death at Bargain Prices
"This is a pretty one of Di at Elstree," says Brian Clemens. "My office was in the building in the background, and that's Stage 5 to the right. Everybody hated Stage 5 – it wasn't well sound-proofed, so if a plane went over you were in trouble. And it had birds nesting in the roof!"

→ Death at Bargain Prices
Steed inspects a toy elephant in Pinters department store.

→→ Death at Bargain Prices
Mrs Peel goes 'undercover' as a sales assistant in the lingerie department. After encountering one of the shop's floorwalkers, Steed tells her, "I asked the chief predator where to find you. He said, 'Our Mrs Peel is in Ladies Underwear.' I rattled up the stairs three at a time."

← **Death at Bargain Prices**
A leather-clad Diana Rigg makes a new friend in the Pinters toy department.

↑ **Death at Bargain Prices**
Fight arranger Ray Austin (left) and wrestler Joe Cornelius are sent flying in pictures ABC used to promote Diana Rigg as "Television's latest guns-and-glamour girl: Emma Peel."

→ **Death at Bargain Prices**
Ray Austin developed a fighting style for Diana Rigg which he dubbed 'Hoaxing'. An October 1965 press release explained: "While having a form all its own, Hoaxing owes something to karate and its deadly chops with the blade of the hand, and also, rather surprisingly, to the angular poses and attitudes of the Hindu deity Shiva – destroyer and reproducer."

↑ Too Many Christmas Trees
"Nothing quite like a Dickensian Christmas!" A publicity still of Diana Rigg and Patrick Macnee taken during the filming of Brandon Storey's fancy dress party. 'Too Many Christmas Trees' eschews seasonal sentimentality for a surreal excursion into telepathic espionage. Notable for some of the most intimate exchanges between Steed and Mrs Peel, as well as some inventive camera work, this episode is the favourite of director Roy Ward Baker.

→ Too Many Christmas Trees
Why the long faces? Roy Ward Baker and Patrick Macnee reflect on the climactic sequence in Brandon Storey's Mirror Room.

↑ **The Cybernauts**
Steed poses as a journalist to visit the "impregnable"
headquarters of United Automation. "The stories
are almost poetically preposterous and superbly
inventive," wrote Monica Furlong, reviewing this
episode for *The Daily Mail* on 15 October 1965.
"Why watch such nonsense? Perhaps because
it *is* nonsense, and it is so nice to be outside the
nightmare instead of inside it."

← The Gravediggers

Following a silent movie-style sequence, Patrick Macnee rescues Diana Rigg from the tracks of the Stapleford Miniature Railway.

→ Room Without a View

Director Roy Ward Baker prepares Patrick Macnee for the scene where Steed takes breakfast at the Chessman Hotel. "I wasn't surprised *The Avengers* appealed to an American audience," says Baker. "It was so damned British, wasn't it? They thought that Steed's bowler hat and brolly were amusing, and of course these things conformed to the stereotypes they held about us. We made very few concessions to them, if any at all. We just made the things the way we thought they should be made.

↓ A Surfeit of H₂O

Mrs Peel dons a PVC fighting suit to investigate Dr Sturm's winery.

← A Surfeit of H2O

Mrs Peel is nearly pulped in Sturm's automated wine press. Between takes, Diana Rigg relaxes on a makeshift head rest.

→ Two's a Crowd

Steed doubles as Gordon Webster, the man who "whips up a soufflé of sartorial surprises". Webster is seen here modelling a lipstick-proof shirt from The Dandy Collection.

↓ Man-eater of Surrey Green

Patrick Macnee enjoys a spot of lunch outside The Surrey Green Arms, in reality The Three Horseshoes in Letchmore Heath. Steed wears a hearing aid in this episode, and its wire can be seen trailing from Macnee's pocket.

← **Silent Dust**
"Don't confuse me with the facts." The stars brush up on the birdwatching references in Roger Marshall's script, which had the working title 'Strictly for the Worms'.

↑ **Silent Dust**
Roy Ward Baker directs the punting sequence on location at Tykes Water Lake in Elstree. "As far as the audience was concerned, Steed and Mrs Peel's relationship was always a bit of a tease," says Baker. "Were they or weren't they having an affair? It remained business-like but it was still extremely sexy."

→ **Silent Dust**
"Tally ho!" Steed gallops to the rescue of Mrs Peel, and Patrick Macnee realises an ambition to ride a horse in the series. Laurence Olivier had ridden the same horse in *Henry V*, over 20 years earlier.

↙ **The Hour That Never Was**

A press release for this episode described Diana Rigg as a "swinging outdoor girl". In this picture she crosses Tykes Water Lake in a pink-and-black trouser suit designed by John Bates.

➜ **The Town Of No Return**

The filming of this episode was partially remounted by director Roy Ward Baker midway through the fourth series, in July 1965. Diana Rigg seamlessly replaced the scenes originally filmed by Elizabeth Shepherd, and the episode was brought to the front of the transmission schedule. Mrs Peel was introduced to viewers in this scene, where Steed drops in on his new partner.

↑ The Town Of No Return
Mrs Peel advises Steed that the cream for his coffee is in the kitchen, and then playfully bars his way. The press were unaware that much of this episode had been filmed so late in the schedule. "Miss Rigg was absolutely at home from the word go," wrote *The Observer*'s Maurice Richardson. "I think I prefer her if anything to her predecessor."

→ The Thirteenth Hole
Mrs Peel practises her putt in a John Bates golfing suit with checked accessories.

→→ The Girl from Auntie
Guest star Liz Fraser poses with Patrick Macnee and Diana Rigg outside Mrs Peel's giant cage.

← **The Danger Makers**
Mrs Peel tackles Major Robertson's
potentially lethal initiation test.

↑ **The Danger Makers**
In November 1965 Patrick Macnee visits
Roger Moore on a neighbouring soundstage
at Elstree. Moore was taking a break from
filming the first colour episode of *The Saint*.

→ **The Danger Makers**
Diana Rigg models the crepe catsuit seen
in this episode. "The pants flare; the
shoulders disappear," exclaimed an
impressed *TV Times*.

↟ **A Touch of Brimstone**
"She is yours, to do with what you will,"
proclaims John Cartney at his Hellfire Club.
Steed appears to be contemplating the offer.

→ **A Touch of Brimstone**
Diana Rigg gets the better of director
James Hill. This episode was never
originally screened in America because it
was considered pornographic by the ABC
network. "However," says a chuckling Brian
Clemens, "I later heard that their executives
used to privately screen it when they got
together for conventions. Even here it was
censored at the time – for the scene at the
end where Peter Wyngarde menaces Di we
had to reduce his whipcracks."

→→ **A Touch of Brimstone**
Diana designed her own costume as the
Queen of Sin. She was less comfortable
with the snake, which spent a day draped
over her wrist.

← The House That Jack Built
Diana Rigg poses with a portrait from 'An Exhibition Dedicated to the Late Emma Peel'.

↑ The House That Jack Built
This episode is well remembered for art director Harry Pottle's eerie sets. Director Don Leaver had made numerous episodes of the videotaped series but excelled with the show's new style and filming techniques.

↗ The House That Jack Built
Pongo hitches a lift to Pendlesham – Diana Rigg and Michael Wynne film a back projection scene in Mrs Peel's Lotus.

→ A Sense of History
Our heroes are joined by Dickie Carlyon (Nigel Stock) at St Bode's fancy dress party. Mrs Peel's Robin Hood is unimpressed by Steed's Sheriff of Nottingham. "That looks a bit droopy," she says, tweaking his sword. "Wait till it's challenged," he replies.

← **How to Succeed .... at Murder**
Diana Rigg surprises her co-star during rehearsals on the set of Henry and Henrietta Throgbottom's keep fit class.

↑ **Honey for the Prince**
In the final black-and-white episode, Steed is prevented from entering Prince Ali's harem. This leaves him no alternative but to ask Mrs Peel, "What size do you take in Turkish trousers?"

→ **Honey for the Prince**
Mrs Peel escapes from the harem with only one of her seven veils intact. "The American network told us they didn't want to see Di's belly button," recalls Brian Clemens. "So we put a jewel in it!"

Series Five

Mrs Peel – We're Needed

Opposite
Patrick Macnee and Diana Rigg
promoted Series Five of *The
Avengers* with this photo shoot
at Lord Montagu of Beaulieu's
private beach.

Right
Diana rode a horse called Tammy
for this September 1966 shoot at
St Mary's Bay in Kent.

Below
This 1967 sales brochure
promised that the new series
would feature "more danger, the
two stars being exposed to every
hazard that ingenuity can devise ...
and it's in colour!"

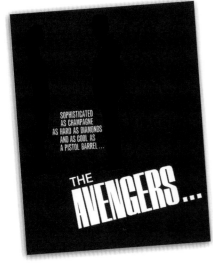

IN AMERICA THE ABC network made the switch to colour programming in 1966. *The Avengers* was expected to follow suit, even though England would not see mainstream colour broadcasting until the end of 1969.

A colour test had been shot on the set of 'Honey for the Prince' in March 1966, but all 24 episodes of Series Five would be filmed with the new process. Albert Fennell and Brian Clemens received a promotion to become the new series' producers, bringing Clemens one step closer to the upper echelons of ABC Television. "They never understood *The Avengers*," he says. "Especially Howard Thomas, who once said to me, 'Why can't we have one set during the Cup Final?' I said to him, 'The Avengers don't go to football matches, and they don't get involved in real things like that.' If we went on location and filmed Patrick queuing up at a bus stop with real people he'd have looked like a pantomime dame. The Avengers had to exist in their own fantasy world, and if someone from real life walked into it the whole thing would have collapsed."

The style of the colour episodes was fine-tuned with the addition of humorous 'tag scenes' at the beginning as well as the end of episodes, although Steed's 'Mrs Peel – We're Needed' introductions would sadly prove to be short-lived.

The programme now relied on American finance, but Clemens doesn't recall any script interference from the ABC network. "Not one bit. Never," he insists. "The Americans regarded *The Avengers* as a house of cards. They were very reluctant to remove one card in case it all fell down. What we did was what Hitchcock had done so magnificently in the 1930s – *The Lady Vanishes* and *The 39 Steps* were unashamedly British pictures but they were so well made that they sold themselves."

To the delight of American audiences the programme continued to depict a rose-tinted view of Olde England and its eccentric criminal masterminds. "It was the England that probably never was, but that we all wish we could go back to," says Clemens. "Of course this particularly applied to the Americans, who seem to think that this country is all about cricket on the village green or fog-shrouded cobbled streets."

The fifth series combined this quintessential Englishness with Carnaby Street chic and a tacit acknowledgement of the more relaxed, liberal values engendered by 1967's Summer of Love. "It was a wonderful era because people weren't getting stabbed in the streets, they were

getting embraced in the streets," says Clemens nostalgically. "But it wasn't just about peace and love. People were discovering champagne, and realising that you could have a brandy after dinner. We exploited all those things. The hippies had a philosophy that you could have a good time without hurting people. We tried to reflect that, but not in a conscious way. If it came through in the programme it was because we felt good."

As before, Clemens also acted as story editor, ensuring a tonal consistency throughout the series. "I would sit next to the writer and we'd

Below
An unconventional steed in this 1967 picture by renowned celebrity photographer Terry O'Neill.

block his script. Once we had the story I'd even sometimes include lines of dialogue. I'd make a copy and then hand it over and say, 'Now go away and write that.' I made a copy in case he got run over by a bus outside the studio. If that happened I'd be able to write the script myself."

Clemens describes a happy, collaborative atmosphere with his writers, but Roger Marshall was less than satisfied with the arrangement. Marshall had contributed some of the finest episodes to Series Three and Four, but now felt stifled by Clemens' omnipotence. He quit the show after delivering just two scripts for Series Five: 'The £50,000 Breakfast' was a remake of his Cathy Gale episode 'Death of a Great Dane', while 'A Funny Thing Happened On The Way To The Station' was rewritten by Clemens and credited to the arch pseudonym 'Brian Sheriff'.

For the launch of the new series the show's stars assumed an even higher profile. Incoming designer Alun Hughes created the classic 'Emmapeeler' catsuit for Diana Rigg, although the rest of his collection didn't quite match the impact of John Bates' designs for Series Four. Patrick Macnee participated in more photo shoots than ever, but in an off guard moment admitted it wasn't really his thing. "I always dress as if I am about to get on a horse," he revealed in April 1967. "Corduroy trousers, no ties, dirty old comfortable boots. I like comfort. Couldn't give a hoot about fashion."

Diana Rigg was similarly focused on her performance, and would receive two Emmy nominations for her efforts. In December 1974 she described her approach to characterisation in an interview with *The Observer*'s Kenneth Harris. "Patrick and I always discussed our parts. We always distinguished between plot and personality. The plot we always swallowed. But we would always discuss, if necessary, personality. We'd get to the studio at 6.30 in the morning and Brian Clemens would give us our script. Whatever the plot, we took it. But as I read the lines, I might say, 'Look, Emma would never say that,' or 'Emma might say that, but not in those words.'"

Diana's second series of *The Avengers* would prove to be her last. She had threatened to resign after Series Four but her loyalty to Patrick Macnee – and the promise of a more equitable salary – convinced her to stay for another year. After leaving the show she resumed her successful stage career and, like her predecessors, took starring roles in feature films. In March 1969 she told *The Daily Sketch*'s Fergus Cashin that, "Emma was destroying me. She dominated me. I woke up in the morning looking at the Avenger bird in the mirror. It was a sort of looking glass war." She has rarely discussed her involvement with the show ever since.

Diana left a programme that was now enjoyed in over 50 countries around the world, although in its native England critics were starting to detect signs of fatigue. In 1967 *The Daily Mail*'s Barry Norman was not alone in noticing that "The formula has become totally predictable now – series of mysterious disappearances, search for link between them, unmasking of master criminal."

The Avengers' British executives also felt it was time for a change. Howard Thomas and ABPC's Robert Norris dismissed Albert Fennell and Brian Clemens in summer 1967. John Bryce, the producer of the latter Honor Blackman episodes, was invited to take control of Series Six.

While it is probably true that *The Avengers* peaked with the black-and-white Emma Peel episodes, the series that followed is only marginally flawed in comparison. Indeed, in terms of repeats and DVD sales, Series Five has proved the most enduring of all. This was illustrated in November 1995 when the *Evening Standard*'s Victor Lewis-Smith devoted his entire column to Channel 4's screening of 'From Venus With Love'. "Dame Diana Rigg is currently playing Mother Courage at the National Theatre," he wrote. "Thirty years ago she was Mrs Courageous on TV, holding the nation spellbound as she battered wrongdoers senseless ... This wasn't the most memorable episode but, as somebody once said about sex, even when it's bad it's wonderful."

Left
Another picture from the St Mary's Bay session. Diana Rigg had learned to ride a horse for the Series Four episode 'Silent Dust'.

Below
A symbol of the computer age tucked in a bowler hat – the red card that grants Steed access to Ministry files in 'The Positive Negative Man'.

Bottom left
Diana wore one of the catsuits designed by Alun Hughes in the first colour episode, 'The Fear Merchants'.

Bottom right
A grey-haired Patrick Macnee returned to Teddington Studios to star in the *Armchair Theatre* production 'The Long Nightmare'. The play was produced by Leonard White and broadcast on 15 October 1966.

✦ In 1966 Alun Hughes took over as Diana Rigg's costume designer. Diana disliked wearing the leather outfits that had been such a predominant feature of Series Three and Four, so Hughes responded with a more feminine wardrobe of suede, silk and chiffon. Hughes' most notable innovation was a range of Crimplene catsuits he called 'Emmapeelers'. "All Emma's clothes are made for movement," he said. "Skirts are easy, dresses have back pleats, coats have a slim line with a back swing."

↑ For Series Five Patrick Macnee was dressed by Italian-born designer Pierre Cardin, whom Macnee and Rigg visited in Paris in January 1967. "I want to bring out the latent dandy in the British male," declared Cardin, who had clearly come to the right place. Cardin's innovations included a striking double-breasted suit, but he essentially followed Macnee's own predilection for Edwardian styling with slim-waisted, flared jackets and close-fitting trousers.

→ The launch of Series Five in January 1967 included a photocall at Teddington Studios. Terry O'Neill photographed Diana Rigg with weightlifter George Manners and racing driver Graham Hill. Patrick Macnee wore a Pierre Cardin mohair evening suit for this picture with swimmer Linda Ludgrove.

The Avengerwear 67 fashion show was held at a Mayfair hotel in January, and unveiled a wide range of designs that were about to go on sale in selected high street stores. The event included a screening of the colour episode 'From Venus With Love' and a catwalk show of 54 outfits with provocative names such as 'Tickety Boo' (a pink linen trouser suit, 10 guineas) and 'Pure Hell' (a white wool evening dress, 18 guineas).

➤ More Terry O'Neill shots from the January photocall at Teddington. The Pierre Cardin dinner suit Patrick Macnee wore in this picture with Twiggy was available from Neville Reed gents' outfitters for £25.

➤➤ Twiggy wears ' Scarface Lil', an Alun Hughes design from the Avengerwear collection. This calf skin coat edged with beige suede was available from the furrier Selincourt for 139 guineas. The outfit was complemented by an 'Emmatopper' hat, 'Grand Slam' stockings, 'Harlequin' gloves and a 'Great Avenger' wristwatch.

➤➤➤ A more traditional Pierre Cardin design for Patrick Macnee in brown wool check, with shepherd check trousers. Twiggy wears an Alun Hughes Ottoman dress named after the episode 'Escape in Time'. The suit was available from the Neville Reed chain, and the dress was on sale at CW Thomas of New Bond Street.

← The Fear Merchants

The British Efficiency Bureau are using
market research to discover the phobias of
leading businessmen – and then using the
information to literally scare them to death.
In the offices of ceramics manufacturer Fox,
White and Crawley, Mrs Peel eavesdrops
on Gordon White being asked some very
unusual questions...

This was the first colour episode into
production in September 1966, and later
became the highest-rated instalment of the
fifth series.

↑ The Fear Merchants

In a deserted quarry Gilbert (Garfield
Morgan) tries to put Steed into the British
Efficiency Bureau's 'dead file'.

→ The Fear Merchants

Steed visits the British Porcelain director
Jeremy Raven (Brian Wilde), and admires
his lesser-billed white-floated crimson
nighthawk. "Charming, quite charming,"
says Steed. "Not quite charming enough,"
remarks the perfectionist Raven, who
promptly smashes it.

↑ Escape in Time
X marks the spot: Mrs Peel follows the trail of some errant criminals by presenting her 'passport' to Anjali (Imogen Hassall).

→ Escape in Time
In a scene that was cited by *The Sunday Telegraph* as the highlight of the episode, Steed handcuffs the villainous Vesta (Judy Parfitt) to a pillar.

→→ Escape in Time
Mrs Peel prepares to be sent back to the 1790s by the wide-eyed and stuttering Waldo Thyssen (Peter Bowles).

↑ The Bird Who Knew Too Much

In a possible acknowledgement of Patrick Macnee's recent forays into modelling, Steed joins Samantha Slade (Ilona Rogers) on an assignment for photographer Tom Savage (Kenneth Cope).

The Times' television critic RW Cooper compared this episode favourably with *The Man from UNCLE* and *Adam Adamant Lives!*, two espionage series screened by the BBC in 1967. Ironically, given that the latter series was created by Sydney Newman in the style of *The Avengers*, Cooper observed that Patrick Macnee "has a touch of the Adam Adamant about him for his debonair eccentricity."

→ The Bird Who Knew Too Much

Patrick Macnee shares a joke with the uncredited Peter Brace before filming Steed's discovery of Percy Danvers' body.

The Bird Who Knew Too Much

Mrs Peel knows a dead parrot when she sees one. Aside from Patrick Macnee, John Wood (seen here as Edgar J Twitter) was the only actor from the original *Avengers* to take part in the ill-fated 1998 film.

From Venus With Love

Barbara Shelley returned to *The Avengers* in the title role of this classic episode, which was the first to be screened when the fifth series began in January 1967.

From Venus With Love

Mrs Peel (played here by Diana Rigg's stunt double Cyd Child) discovers the real source of the Venusian attacks, but is soon assailed by the machine's operator Martin (Joe Powell).

From Venus With Love

Mrs Peel is restrained as insane optician Dr Primble aims his laser at her. "Subliminally it was quite kinky," says Diana Rigg of *The Avengers*. "I always seemed to be strapped to a dentist's chair with my feet in the air."

→ The See-Through Man
In a scene that didn't make the finished programme, Major Alexandre Vazin inspects the notes in Quilby's laboratory.

→→ The See-Through Man
"Invisible man? I would see through that one immediately!" This episode marked Warren Mitchell's second appearance as the hapless Soviet ambassador Vladimir Brodny.

↓ The Winged Avenger
A comic book character is brought to life as a killer with steel talons. In the gravity-defying climax Mrs Peel wrestles with the masked murderer on the ceiling.

↟ **The Hidden Tiger**
Production designer Robert Jones'
remarkable set for Furry Lodge,
the headquarters of PURRR
(the Philanthropic Union for the
Rescue, Relief and Recuperation
of Cats).

→ **The Hidden Tiger**
The "lost, neglected and homeless"
souls of PURR were provided by
animal trainer John Holmes, who
brought them from his farm in
Dorset. Holmes stayed in a caravan
during filming, while the cats were
given a specially fitted dressing
room at Elstree.

← The Superlative Seven
The crew film a close-up as one of Kanwitch and Jessel's killers steps forward to take a deadly aptitude test.

↙ The Superlative Seven
Steed is left a sitting duck as his fellow party guests mistakenly accuse him of murder.

↓ The Superlative Seven
Terry Plummer, dressed as Oriental wrestler Toy Sung, prepares to film the opening scene. In the background Donald Sutherland waits for his cue.

↖ The Correct Way to Kill
Brian Clemens used his own script for Series Three's 'The Charmers' as the inspiration for this episode. This time round Steed was partnered with Soviet agent Olga Valovski, played by Anna Quayle. Also pictured is director Charles Crichton, who had made his name at Ealing Studios in the 1940s and would go on to direct *A Fish Called Wanda*.

←← Epic
Steed saves Mrs Peel from a split personality. "This episode came about because we were running slightly over-budget," says Clemens. "To save money I said I'd write one that took place in a film studio! It's now something of a museum piece, because it shows you almost the whole of ABPC Elstree."

← Epic
Diana Rigg takes a break from filming ZZ Von Schnerk's 'The Destruction of Mrs Emma Peel' on the Elstree backlot.

← The Superlative Seven

Brian Clemens recycled elements from another of his Honor Blackman scripts, 'Dressed to Kill', for this episode, which similarly begins with Steed lured to a fancy dress party on false pretences. In this scene he meets Mrs Hana Wilde (Charlotte Rampling) aboard the aeroplane where the party is to be held. Clemens liked the character's name so much he called Steed's partner Mrs Hannah Wild in his short-lived *Avengers* stage play of 1971.

↑ A Funny Thing Happened On The Way To The Station

"Another five miles Mr Steed," says the Ticket Inspector, "and then…"
"Pop goes the diesel?" suggests Steed. Fortunately he is able to free himself in time to prevent the Prime Minister being assassinated on a train.

↗ Something Nasty in the Nursery

A hypnotised Sir George Collins (Patrick Newell) clutches a baby bouncer from GONN – the sinister Guild of Noble Nannies. Newell would return to the series in the regular role of Steed's boss Mother.

↓ **Return of the Cybernauts**
↓ **Return of the Cybernauts**
The robot assassins were resurrected for a colour sequel in 1967. "I love men with big shoulders," coos secretary Rosie (Aimi MacDonald) before a Cybernaut (Terry Richard) casually sweeps her aside.

↘ **Return of the Cybernauts**
"He's had some kind of nervous breakdown." Steed puts an end to the Cybernauts' latest scheme.

← **The Joker**
A stunning portrait of Diana Rigg from this episode, which was a remake of the Series Three story 'Don't Look Behind You'. In 2008 Diana told *The Daily Telegraph*'s Nigel Farndale, "I sometimes think, when I look back on those days: why didn't I have more confidence? Why didn't I know I was pretty good-looking?"

↑ **Dead Man's Treasure**
George Benstead (Arthur Lowe) demonstrates his race track simulator but forgets to tell Steed that there is a shocking penalty for mistakes.

♠ You Have Just Been Murdered

Mrs Peel's leather catsuit made its only Series Five appearance during this sequence, in which Nicholls (Frank Maher) prevents her recovering a suitcase of blackmail money.

↗ The Positive Negative Man

Steed fishes for information from Top Hush secretary Cynthia Wentworth-Howe (Caroline Blakiston). This scene, like the one in the preceding picture, was filmed on location at Tykes Water Lake in Elstree.

→ Mission … Highly Improbable

A tiny Steed clambers out of a miniaturised Saracen armoured car and hides on Shaffer's desk. When Shaffer has left the room, Steed calls Mrs Peel on a relatively giant telephone. "What's happened to you?" she asks. "If I told you, you wouldn't believe it," he replies.

↓ Mission … Highly Improbable

Choking on the smoke from Shaffer's cigar, Steed knocks it into the bottom of an ashtray.

↟ The Forget-Me-Knot

"Always keep your bowler on in times of stress.
And watch out for diabolical masterminds. Goodbye Steed."
Mrs Peel kisses Steed on the cheek and prepares to join
her waiting husband. She turns to leave and Steed says,
"Emma ... Thanks."

Diana Rigg's final episode was actually filmed from
December 1967 to January 1968, well into the production
schedule of the sixth series. 'The Forget-Me-Knot' was
written by Brian Clemens over a frantic weekend, and
became the only episode of *The Avengers* to feature a
handover between Steed's partners. "I wrote it so Steed
both lost and got the girl," says Clemens. Diana Rigg
returned for several days' filming, which included Mrs
Peel's poignant farewell and an encounter with her
replacement on the stairs outside Steed's flat.

Series Six

Agent 69

IN 1967 IT WAS ANNOUNCED that John Bryce would be taking over from Albert Fennell and Brian Clemens as the producer of *The Avengers*. "There will be changes, too, in the approach to storylines in future *Avengers* scripts," said an article in the 15 July edition of trade magazine *Kine Weekly*. "The way-out story is to be replaced by a more realistic type of tale with an emphasis on tension and excitement in place of light-hearted plotting."

The news was poorly received by the crew of the final Diana Rigg episodes. "I can't remember anybody at Elstree agreeing with the decision to take Albert and Brian off the show," says second unit director John Hough. "It just didn't make any sense at all. Along with Laurie Johnson, who composed the music, they were an essential part of *The Avengers*."

John Bryce's first task was to find a replacement for Diana Rigg. Around 200 actresses attended the original audition, and this was whittled down to a shortlist of just three: the English Mary Peach, the American Tracy Reed and the Canadian Linda Thorson. The 20 year-old Thorson was considered in need of a make-over, so her hair was dyed blonde and she was sent to the Henlow Grange health farm to lose

weight while the executives at America's ABC network considered her screen test. "When they told me I had the part I hadn't had anything but hot water and lemon for eight days and I fainted with the excitement," she says. "After that the photographers arrived and it all began."

Bryce planned to take the role of the *Avengers* heroine in a new direction. "I think it's time to go back to femininity," he told *The Daily Mail* on 30 October 1967. "We've had all the leather business – the new girl will essentially be a woman. She will be soft with all the female weaknesses – and attributes."

Unlike her predecessors, Linda's character, 'Agent 69', would be a member of Steed's own organisation, albeit a rookie with no experience in the field. Linda herself came up with a patriotic-sounding name for the new girl – Tara King.

Linda's first episode, the 90-minute 'Invitation to a Killing', was directed by Robert Asher in late 1967. Linda had lost weight, as requested, but the peroxide used to bleach her hair had caused much of it to fall out. As a result she would spend months in a variety of wigs, beginning with a conspicuous blonde number. John Hough returned to the show as second unit director, and remembers a fraught atmosphere during the early episodes. "Diana was a difficult act to

Left
Patrick Macnee and Linda Thorson meet the press at a Thames-side photocall on 20 October 1967.

Below
The sales brochure for *The Avengers*' sixth and final series.

Right
Tara King, novice Agent 69, brushes up on her cryptanalysis in 'Get-a-Way!'

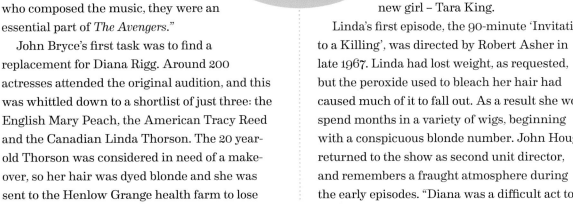

follow," he says. "I think Linda knew the only way to go was to be totally different from her, but she was thrown in at the deep end and there weren't enough people to help her. They weren't even sure what clothes she should wear, or what her hairstyle should be."

Hough also missed the guidance of his former producers. "Albert and Brian weren't just interested in how quickly you shot something, they were just as interested in *how* you shot something. All the conversations I had with them were about artistry. They schooled the directors, challenging us to come up with something that surprised and interested them. *The Avengers* was the only television series I worked on at that time where this happened. Those sorts of conversations stopped when they left the show, but fortunately they weren't gone for very long."

The first three episodes produced by Bryce were considered so disappointing that he was fired. A contrite ABC Television asked Brian Clemens to return, which he agreed to do on the condition that Albert Fennell was also reinstated. "They let John go for what I thought were a lot of spurious reasons," says Linda. "He was a great

producer and they didn't give him anything like a chance. I wept and wept when he left because I loved him. I just couldn't bear it. I was only 20 years old and had just moved to England. I was alone in a country where I didn't have a husband, a father, an uncle, a solicitor, a dentist or a doctor. I just kept thinking, What the hell is happening?"

Fennell and Clemens reasserted themselves by bringing Diana Rigg back for a handover episode, 'The Forget-Me-Knot', and salvaging what they could from the footage Bryce had already shot. A new dynamic emerged between Patrick Macnee and Linda Thorson – Steed became a more paternal mentor and Tara became his admiring, slightly infatuated apprentice. "As soon as we came in we expressed Linda's strengths," says Clemens. "We couldn't have her aping Di Rigg, so we put a brick in her handbag and all that sort of thing."

In 'The Forget-Me-Knot' Clemens introduced a new regular character in the shape of the rotund Mother, played by Patrick Newell. Steed and Tara's crippled boss was soon joined by the statuesque Rhonda (Rhonda Parker), who wheeled him to numerous eccentric rendezvous

Below
Filming of the second version of the Series Six title sequence began during production of the episode 'False Witness' in July 1968. This scene with Linda Thorson was shot on location at Aldenham Park in Elstree.

Below right
"I look like I need to get some sleep!" says Brian Clemens of this picture, which was taken towards the end of production in 1969.

with his agents. "I created Mother because Linda was Canadian, so I thought we needed somebody who could bounce the humour off Steed," says Clemens. "I didn't believe that Steed and Tara could have the same kind of interchange, and that's the reason Mother's there. It's been said that he was there at the request of the American network, but it was nothing to do with that."

"I loved working with Paddy Newell, but I thought Mother was an embellishment," says Linda. "It seemed to me that he was there because there was a loss of confidence in the partnership between the man and the woman."

Under Clemens' control, the sixth series utterly thwarted Bryce's original ambitions. New heights of glorious lunacy were scaled with the jaw-dropping 'Look – (stop me if you've heard this one before) But There Were These Two Fellers...', written by Dennis Spooner. Former stunt arranger Ray Austin directed the outstanding 'All Done With Mirrors' and John Hough contributed the excellent 'Super Secret Cypher Snatch' and three further episodes. Robert Jones' set designs became increasingly psychedelic, helping to lend the sixth series a unique identity. More than ever, Steed and his partner's missions resembled a surreal game. "We were in our own time and space, almost as if *The Avengers* took place on an island," says Linda. "It was marvellously unpredictable, full of serendipity and madness."

After its teething problems, the sixth series represented something of a return to form. Brian Clemens now considers it "the best series in terms of scripts, and it certainly didn't do any worse than the Diana Rigg episodes in terms of income."

In America, ABC were confident enough to regard *The Avengers* as a valuable weapon in the ratings war with rival NBC. "We are still the only British television series ever to play in prime time on an American network," says Clemens. "That was our accolade and our undoing. ABC put us opposite *Rowan & Martin's Laugh-In*. It was the biggest show on American television, and we couldn't compete with that. If they'd given us a different slot we might still be running today."

Although *The Avengers* continued to be successful around the world, a slide in American ratings condemned the series to cancellation. The

final episode was produced and broadcast in 1969. It went under the appropriate title 'Bizarre'.

The Avengers was over but, 50 years after it began, it enjoys a reputation as perhaps the greatest of all cult series from a golden age of television. "It's a classic which still holds up well today," says John Hough. "I'm very proud to have been a part of it."

Linda Thorson is similarly pleased that the memory of the show lives on. "Everything's done in such a rush now, but we had a good budget, some great guest stars and at least two weeks to shoot every episode. Above all, we had *fun*. *The Avengers* was the best of the best."

Top

Linda Thorson is still smoking her cigarette in this rehearsal for the original Series Six titles. The sequence was directed by Harry Booth at Elstree in January 1968.

Above

"I think I got the role because I wanted it more than any other actress in the world," says Linda.

Left

The curtain falls: second unit director John Hough (second from left) and Patrick Macnee (far right) join the crew on the Elstree backlot for the filming of the final episode, 'Bizarre'.

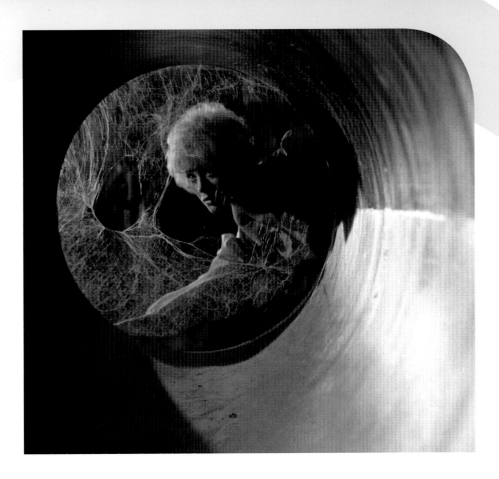

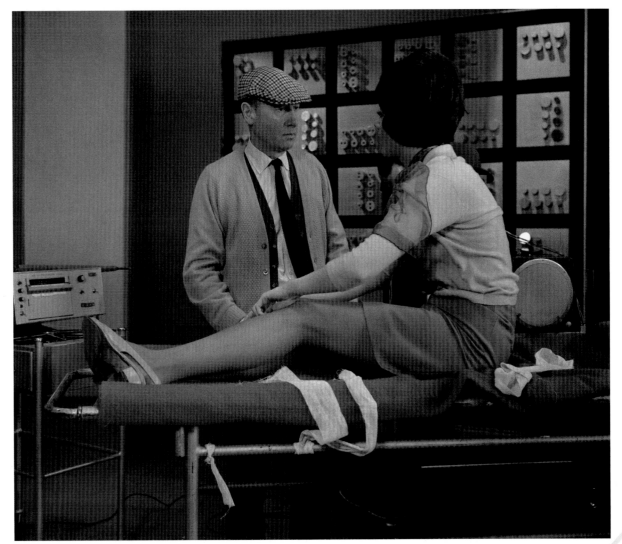

◄◄ **Invasion of the Earthmen**
"We inherited a few episodes from John
Bryce, but the only one that was half
good was Terry Nation's 'Invasion of
the Earthmen'," says Brian Clemens.
"We made a few changes and kept that one."

In this scene, Tara spots a strange
creature in the grounds of the Alpha
Academy, a militaristic training school
for astronauts.

↖ **Invasion of the Earthmen**
In 1968 *The Times'* Henry Rayner
described Steed's new partner, Tara King,
as "an innocently impertinent charmer
who suggests a different sort of kinky
eccentricity from that exploited by either
of her predecessors."

↑ **Split!**
At the Nullington private hospital
Dr Constantine prepares to transfuse
the mind and personality of Boris
Kartovski into Tara.

← **Split!**
Director Roy Ward Baker rehearses
Linda Thorson for the scene where Steed
rescues Tara from the operating table.

◄◄ Get-a-Way!

Patrick Macnee is flanked by camera operator Peter Elvin and clapper boy Peter Taylor. An Add-a-Vision monitor on the camera dolly allows the rest of the crew to see the scene as shot by Elvin. In February 1968 Don Sharp, the director of this episode, told *Kine Weekly* that the new Add-a-Vision system had allowed him to turn his back on an actual take and work from one of the monitors. Appreciative director of photography Gilbert Taylor added: "It saves you screwing yourself up into a tiny space close to the set."

▲ Get-a-Way!

Patrick Macnee and Linda Thorson consult Don Sharp about the scene where Steed and Tara puzzle over a copy of *Bryant's Natural History Magazine*. "Don was lovely to work with," says Linda, "and I enjoyed our grown-up conversations. He told you exactly what he wanted and then made it happen."

◄ Have Guns – Will Haggle

Trapped inside an armoury that is about to explode, Tara anxiously waits for Steed to rescue her. Fortunately the large safety pin on her tartan skirt enables him to pick the lock of her handcuffs in record time.

← Look – (stop me if you've heard this one) But There Were These Two Fellers…

Harvey Gould had designed Linda Thorson's costumes at the beginning of Series Six, but by February 1968 Alun Hughes had returned with a new portfolio. This included several variations on the culottes that became something of a Tara King trademark.

↑ Look – (stop me if you've heard this one) But There Were These Two Fellers…

Linda studies her script on the set of Sir Jeremy Broadfoot's office. Behind her are (left to right) co-producer Brian Clemens, continuity girl June Randall and director James Hill.

↗ Look – (stop me if you've heard this one) But There Were These Two Fellers…

Killer clown 'Merrie' Maxie Martin (Jimmy Jewel, right) visits gag writer Bradley Marler (Bernard Cribbins) in an office waist-deep in discarded jokes.

  The Daily Mail's Virginia Ironside described this episode as "by far the best *Avengers* story I've seen … It wasn't just the sharp touches in the script by Dennis Spooner that made it; the direction was perfect, full of original ideas and elaborate quick change disguise effects."

→ Look – (stop me if you've heard this one) But There Were These Two Fellers…

The year before *Monty Python's Flying Circus* started, John Cleese pioneered his silly walk in this cameo as Marcus Rugman, a civil servant who maintains a registry of clown make-ups painted on eggs.

← **My Wildest Dream**
It's for you – Patrick Macnee rehearses a scene in the hospital observation department.

↙ **My Wildest Dream**
Linda Thorson rehearses part of the same sequence wearing a pair of her own dark glasses.

→ **My Wildest Dream**
With colour television established in America and just around the corner in Britain, Alun Hughes was mindful of the fact that his designs were increasingly being seen very differently. "I must think in terms of this at all times," he said in 1968. "I have to know how much colour actually comes over on the screen. And sometimes colours can appear differently during interior scenes shot under strong studio lighting than in scenes set outdoors."

↤ My Wildest Dream

The Avengers' co-producer Albert Fennell, pictured here with Linda Thorson on the set of Aloyisius Peregrine's flat. "Albert was very compassionate and very good to me," says Linda. "He was a gentleman, and I'm very sad he's no longer with us."

↟ Whoever Shot Poor George Oblique Stroke XR40?

Tara infiltrates the home of computer genius Sir Wilfred Pelley posing as his niece, Prunella. Linda reverted to her native Canadian accent and adopted a 1930s look for Tara's ruse.

↗ Whoever Shot Poor George Oblique Stroke XR40?

Patrick Macnee has revealed that both he and Linda Thorson were prescribed the amphetamine Durophet as an aid to weight loss. The results were dramatic, although Macnee suffered worse side effects than his co-star and later struggled to kick the drug. Macnee also regrets the sideburns he grew during 1968, which he now considers "made me look like a back street dealer in pornographic magazines."

➔ You'll Catch Your Death

"Love the guy, hate my hair!" says Linda of this shot, which she shared with director of photography Alan Hume. A mainstay of the Carry On films, Hume later worked on three James Bond movies and such classics as *A Fish Called Wanda* and *Shirley Valentine*.

→ All Done With Mirrors

Director Ray Austin briefs Linda Thorson for the scene where Tara visits Miss Emily. This was Austin's first episode as a fully-fledged director, although he had been the stunt arranger on both Emma Peel series and had directed the additional footage that had transformed the unscreened Tara King pilot 'Invitation to a Killing' into 'Have Guns – Will Haggle'. "Ray was a natural," says Linda. "A confident man who brought that confidence to every aspect of his work as a director."

→ All Done With Mirrors

Linda Thorson perches on the AC 428 Convertible driven by Tara in eight episodes of Series Six. The car had been introduced as Steed's vehicle in 'Invasion of the Earthmen', before returning producers Albert Fennell and Brian Clemens put him behind the wheel of a vintage Rolls-Royce.

✦ All Done With Mirrors

One of the sixth series' best episodes, 'All Done With Mirrors' saw a
role reversal as Tara is dispatched on a mission with an inexperienced
male agent. At the end of the episode Tara emerges from a watery grave
and sends a message to Steed from the lamp room of Colonel Withers'
lighthouse. "Don't worry, I won't haunt you," she tells Steed, "... if you
promise to take me out for dinner tonight."

Alun Hughes designed a hard-wearing denim outfit for Linda Thorson,
to meet the demands of this episode's vigorous location sequences.

← All Done With Mirrors

Linda passed her driving test in Toronto and then had to come to terms with right-hand drive vehicles when she started making *The Avengers* in England. She drove a Lotus Elan in 'Have Guns – Will Haggle', but accidentally ran the vehicle into a wall during filming. She felt more comfortable with the AC 428, which was an automatic, and eventually bought a left-hand drive Mustang.

→ Super Secret Cypher Snatch

Disguised as Fred from the Classy Glass Cleaning Co, Steed breaks into HQ Cypher Division and removes the headset that is feeding Tara tape-recorded hypnosis.

"The programme – arguably the best series produced by British television – is as good as ever," said *The Times'* Julian Critchley, reviewing this episode. "It is as camp as a row of tents, which is how we like it nowadays."

↓ Super Secret Cypher Snatch

Director John Hough demonstrates the giant props that enabled him to frame a shot of Tara through the handle of a tea cup. Hough made his directorial debut with this episode, but handled the second unit throughout Series Six.

↘ Super Secret Cypher Snatch

"This is how they did it," says Tara, realising that photographer Peters was shot by someone outside the building. "Foresight," replies Steed. "It's not every assassin who carries his own ladder."

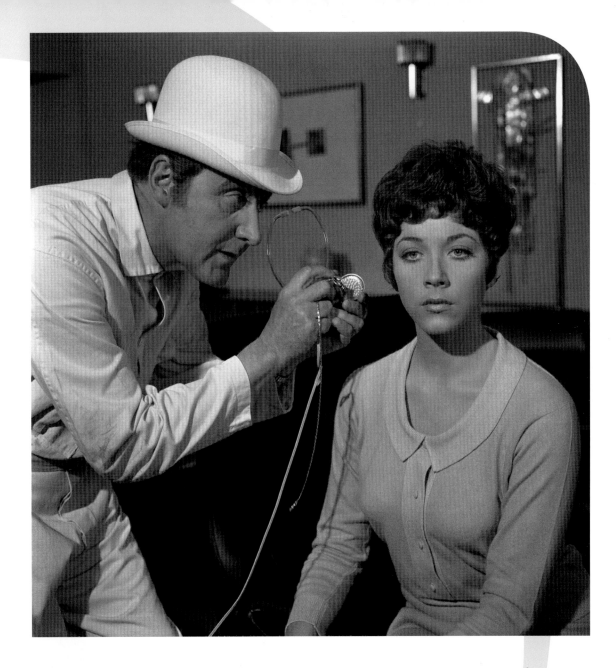

↑ **Game**
The 'Game' unit pose on location at the children's playground where Steed and Tara find Dexter's body. Director Robert Fuest (in a white sweater, standing behind Macnee and Thorson) had served as a production designer on *The Avengers*' first series in 1961.

→ **Game**
Cornered by Steed and Tara, Monty Bristow (Peter Jeffrey) uses his ultimate weapon: a playing card with a razor-sharp edge.

→→ **Game**
Steed drove a 1923 Rolls-Royce Silver Ghost in this and 17 other episodes in Series Six. Patrick Macnee missed the Bentleys he had previously driven. "The Bentley was in keeping with Steed's character," he says. "He wouldn't have been so ostentatious as to have had a Rolls."

→ **False Witness**
Tara's sabotage of the hallucinatory milk at Dreemykreem Dairies is interrupted by Sykes (John Bennett), who locks her inside a butter machine.

↓ **Noon Doomsday**
Seven years on from the day and hour he was convicted, a vengeful Gerald Kafka (Peter Bromilow) levels his guns at an incapacitated Steed. Tara is pinned to a door with a knife, unable to help.

↘ **Noon Doomsday**
Director Peter Sykes filmed this parody of *High Noon* on location at Brian Clemens' Bedfordshire farm in July 1968. Linda Thorson wore her 'Noon Doomsday' outfit in the second version of the Series Six title sequence, which was directed by Robert Fuest and John Hough during the schedule for this and the previous episode, 'False Witness'.

◄◄ Legacy of Death
On the Elstree backlot director Don Chaffey rehearses the scene where Steed and Tara find the unconscious Klaus (Alf Joint). Chaffey had previously directed *One Million Years B.C.* for Hammer, and would go on to make the Disney film *Pete's Dragon*.

◄ Legacy of Death
Steed practises flying a model aeroplane he is making for his nephew's tenth birthday. "When's that?" asks Tara. "Three years ago," he replies. "The instructions are very hard to follow."

↑ They Keep Killing Steed
Patrick Newell was a mainstay of the sixth series as Steed and Tara's boss, Mother. "Although it's not much fun having everyone call me 'Mother' the part is so good that it is worth it," he said in 1968.

← Wish You Were Here
Tara studies a postcard from her Uncle Charles and decides he has been on holiday at the Elizabethan Hotel for a suspiciously long time. This sophisticated *homage* to *The Prisoner* was directed by Don Chaffey, who had recently made some of the key episodes of that series.

↑ Killer

Linda Thorson was on holiday in September 1968 so for much of this episode Steed was partnered by Lady Diana Forbes-Blakeney, played by the 24 year-old Jennifer Croxton. In this picture, director Cliff Owen rehearses the scene where 'Forbes' reminds Steed of Agents' Manual Section Three Paragraph Four: "Always go in through a skylight."

➤ Killer

"I've got this face – it's not pretty and it's not plain either," Jennifer Croxton told the *TV Times*' Eithne Power in January 1969. "Friends say it's a Jennifer Croxton face." She expressed the hope that her appearance in 'Killer' would provide a boost to her career. "I must say I'm looking forward to being a success at 25."

➤➤ The Rotters

Tara regains consciousness and finds herself chained to a wall. Could a nearby bottle of pyrochloric acid provide a solution?

← The Interrogators
"Of course we do try to make their stay as pleasant as possible." Master torturer Colonel Mannering (Christopher Lee) enrols Tara on the TOHE (Test of Human Endurance) course.

↙ The Morning After
In the middle of a ghost town, Steed and television reporter Jenny Firston (Penelope Horner) search for Tara but find Sergeant Hearn (Brian Blessed) waiting for them.

↓ Love All
Steed saves a lovesick Tara from jumping out of a window. Patrick Macnee didn't realise it at the time, but he injured himself during the filming of this scene. "I raced to the window and cracked three or four ribs," he remembers. "I was trying to make the scene as realistic as possible. Stupid, really, since Linda's feet were only a few feet from the studio floor!"

→ Love All
Steed and Tara learn about Mother's latest sticky wicket – a security leak at the Department of Missile Redeployment. Mother's dutiful assistant Rhonda (Rhonda Parker) helps him with his pads.

↑ **Take Me To Your Leader**
Director Robert Fuest (right) leads a jovial rehearsal of the scene where Mother, Tara, Steed and forensics expert Major Glasgow (Henry Stamper) examine an X-ray of a talking briefcase.

→ **Fog**
Linda Thorson with John Hough, the director of this episode. "I adored John," says Linda. "He was wonderful with actors and he really took time with me."

→ → **Fog**
On the trail of the Gaslight Ghoul, Tara joins Mother in the specially adapted Mini Moke he and Rhonda are using to navigate London's fogbound streets.

←← **Who Was That Man I Saw You With?**
Linda Thorson is filmed for the scene where her attempted sabotage of the mysterious 'Field Marshal' is discovered.

← **Who Was That Man I Saw You With?**
"You'll be pleased to know that I've now tried to destroy this room four times, and each time I've failed miserably," Tara tells General Hesketh (Ralph Michael) and Gilpin (Alan MacNaughtan).

↓ **Pandora**
Rhonda Parker relaxes between takes on the set of this episode. The Australian actress appeared in 18 episodes of Series Six but was never given any dialogue, or a credit.

→ **Thingumajig**
"Tara King has a nice round-eyed sense of comedy," said *The Sun*'s Nancy Banks-Smith. "She does a far more probable woman than Cathy Gale or Emma Peel."

← Homicide and Old Lace

A patchwork of flashbacks framed by new
sequences of Mother telling a story to two
of his aunts, 'Homicide and Old Lace' is one
of the most unusual episodes in the entire
series. It largely comprises footage from the
abandoned John Bryce-produced episode 'The
Great Great Britain Crime', including this
scene of Tara cracking Colonel Corf's safe.

↑ Requiem

Guest star Angela Douglas, in costume as a
fancy dress tramp, heads to 'Fort Steed' with
Patrick Macnee.

→ Bizarre

"Are our angels dolly enough for you?"
Macnee rehearses the scene where Steed
takes advantage of the hospitality offered by a
haven for embarrassed financiers.

Bizarre

The last episode of *The Avengers* finished filming on 3 March 1969, and Patrick Macnee admits he shed a tear at the wrap party.

In the final scene Steed shows Mother and Tara a rocket he has constructed in his back yard. Mother leaves to take a photograph, and Tara presses the launch button. The rocket takes off, and she is alone with Steed at last. Mother reassures viewers that they'll be back, before exclaiming "They're unchaperoned up there!"

A stoic press release acknowledged the end of an era: "The running has had to stop for the urbane John Steed. No more will his steel bowler bop, no longer will he hold the ungodly at bay with his brolly. 'Never mind,' he sighs, 'we all of us had a jolly good run. And another thing ... do you think there are any diabolical masterminds on Mars?'

"On a rocket bound for the Valhalla of all television heroes, the Avengers leave us as we so often have left them. Laughing..."

Episode index